THE ELECTRONIC CAMPUS
an information strategy

edited by
Lynne J. Brindley

Proceedings of a conference held on 28-30 October 1988 at
Banbury

Library and Information Research Report 73

Production Note

The majority of scripts in this publication were received in typewritten form. A Kurzweil Document Reader 'learns' the various type faces and sizes used in order to convert the printed page into computer ASCII text. The text processing package LaTeX assembles the pages and generates the contents pages. LaTeX runs on a variety of computer systems from the lowly Atari ST to the largest mainframe system. On this occasion, for convenience a DEC VAX processor was employed.

Textual material was also input from Apple Mac software, files being trans-ferred to the VAX by means of Kermit running on an IBM PC reading the Mac disks on an Apple Macintosh II across a TOPS network. Diagrams were pre-pared using Illustrator 88 on the Apple Macintosh II and the resulting postscript code was incorporated in the relevant place in the source text. The landscape figure was created in MACwrite, scaled using Quark Express and incorporated into the relevant place in source text.

Proof reading output was printed on an Apple Laserwriter and minor page layout adjustment made using the program DVItoVDU on the VAX. Camera-ready copy was 'printed' on a Linotron 300 (a phototypesetter working at 2450 dots per inch via a RIP II (raster image processor which accepts postscript input) which is connected to the university network.

R&DD/C/112

Library and Information Research Reports are published by the British Library Board and distributed by the British Library Publications Sales Unit, Boston Spa, Wetherby, West Yorkshire LS23 7BQ, UK. In the USA they are distributed by the American Library Association, 50 East Huron Street, Chicago, Illinois 60611. In Japan they are distributed by Kinokuniya Co Ltd, PO Box 55, Chi-tose, Tokyo 156. In India, Burma, Pakistan, Nepal, Bangladesh and Sri Lanka they are distributed by Arnold Publishers (India) Private Ltd, AB/9 First Floor, Safdarjang Enclave, New Delhi 110029.

Printed in Great Britain at the University Press, Cambridge.

THE ELECTRONIC CAMPUS
an information strategy

Charles Seale-Hayne Library

University of Plymouth

(01752) 588 588

LibraryandITenquiries@plymouth.ac.uk

British Library Cataloguing in Publication Data
The Electronic campus: an information strategy:
proceedings of a conference held on 28–30 October
1988 at Banbury. – (Library information research
report, ISSN 0263-1709; 73)
1. Higher education institutions. Libraries.
Information services. Technological innovation
I. Brindley, Lynne II. Series
025.5'2777

ISBN 0-7123-3187-5

The Editor

Lynne Brindley is the Director of Library & Information Services at Aston
University, Birmingham. She spent most of her earlier professional career
at the British Library, holding the posts of Head of Marketing and Support
for Bibliographic Services, and Head of the Chief Executive's Office, where
she was responsible for the coordination of the British Library's first strategic
plan. In 1985 she moved to Aston and in 1987 took on the additional role of
Pro-Vice-Chancellor for Information Technology, with strategic responsibility
for information systems and services across the campus. She has written and
spoken widely on the electronic campus, and has recently become Chairman of
the Sconul Automation Policy Committee, and a member of the British Library
Research and Development Department's Advisory Committee.

Abstract

The Electronic Campus: an information strategy presents the proceedings of a conference sponsored by the British Library Research and Development Department, held at Banbury on 28-30 October 1988.

The conference brought together an invited group of senior policy- and decision-makers, academics, librarians, and computing directors, some attending as institutional teams, others as individuals. The aims were to explore key issues for the future information environment of the electronic campus, to share experience and to create greater awareness of developments in the UK and the USA.

The papers focus on the implications of information technology (IT) for the nature and methods of teaching and research, across all disciplines. Economic issues of the new information systems and services are explored from a publishing and from a library perspective. Organisational implications of the electronic campus are discussed, in terms of both the possible re-definition of roles and the wider need for an IT strategy in a distributed information environment. Strategic planning for information resources and an extensive overview of trends in IT complete the thematic papers.

These are complemented by four case studies of computer-intensive campuses in the UK, showing very different approaches to developments. The conference provided ample time for syndicate groups and general discussion, and the main points are summarised.

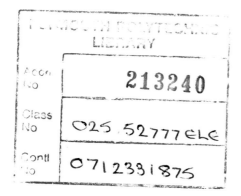

Contents

vi

Foreword

Brian J. Perry, *Director of the British Library Research and Development Department*

For several years the British Library Research and Development Department has given priority to the support of research in the application of information technology (IT), particularly with regard to the implications for the future development of libraries and their services, electronic publishing and the pattern of scholarly research. From the results of our research, and the analysis of trends, it has become increasingly evident that technology is drawing together the retrieval, storage and communication of information of all kinds, whether this is undertaken by libraries, researchers and educators, or managers and administrators. This electronic confluence of information is developing in a variety of contexts, including higher education.

Because of these trends, the Department decided to sponsor the conference on 'The Electronic Campus – an Information Strategy', held at Banbury in October 1988. The conference brought together senior policy- and decision-makers, academics and librarians, some of whom were already well advanced in their thinking in this area, to explore the areas of the future information environment, to share their experiences and their visions, and to prepare to take a lead in developments and strategy planning at institutional level. A similar conference was held at Wingspread in the USA in 1986, and we were fortunate in persuading some of the participants in this US conference to come to Banbury, thus enabling us to bring together the best of British and American experience. A series of position papers was prepared, and case studies of several 'computer-intensive' campuses were presented. Time was allowed for plenary and syndicate discussions, which proved particularly valuable. Some participants were invited to attend the conference as a team from their institution, others were invited as individuals, because of the special skills or perspectives that they could bring.

The event proved to be timely and successful, and heightened our understanding of many of the issues involved in this exciting future. It also pointed up the scope for further research. My thanks go to the Conference Organising Committee, my colleagues in the Department, who ensured that the plans went without a hitch, and to Lynne Brindley, who so successfully edited the proceedings on our behalf, and finally to Peter Abbott, Acting Director of Computer Services at Aston University, who bravely volunteered to undertake the electronic publication of the text.

I commend this publication to all who are interested in the various concerns discussed at the conference, and would be grateful to receive any comments from readers who may feel that a further conference would be desirable.

Editor's Introduction

The key driving force behind the organisation of the conference, and underpinning its agenda, is the recognition of the challenge posed by developments in information and communication technology to academics, and the academic way of life. Educational imperatives of the past are increasingly being questioned as information technology offers the potential to transform teaching and learning methods. Academics inform and teach through lectures, articles, books and so on. Using IT can make this process more effective, but it requires a grasp of the integrative power of systems, which can link TV, video, computers and large databases, giving the ability to access and chart routes through a wealth of knowledge, newly presented. New student learning methods can open up interactions beyond traditional contact with academic tutors, through learning by interaction with computers, other students, wherever they happen to be studying, and beyond, with businessmen and industrialists. For libraries, traditionally central to the learning and research process, there are opportunities for changing approaches to information processing, to the harnessing of information resources, and to the delivery of information services.

In the formulation of an academic strategy for the information age it is important to focus institutional planning efforts on information requirements and systems. There is a need for integrated planning (involving academic departments, central and local administrative functions, major academic services, the Computing Centre, the Library, and communication resources), to make the most of the convergence of technologies, and to ensure most benefit from investment in IT. For these reasons the Banbury conference was organised, to expose decision-makers to the issues that could so dramatically change the future of their institutions.

The implications of IT for the nature and methods of teaching and research are at the core of the conference. In teaching, IT is creating new study media – interactive video, cable and satellite TV, computer-assisted learning packages which are helping students to learn on their own and which bring new opportunities for innovation in distance learning. Gardner in his paper rightly points out that the electronic campus will not of its own accord bring about improvements in the quality of teaching. He describes the contribution of the Computers in Teaching Initiative (CTI) in pointing up the wider issues, such as the changing nature of interpersonal relationships, caused by new learning techniques, as well as providing a range of examples of good software for teaching. The programme clearly demonstrated that the technology has a place across the full breadth of the curriculum, with examples ranging from classics to clinical medical education, providing discipline-specific insights into the learning process. The need for a national programme to recognise, disseminate and reward the production of quality educational software is raised.

The impact of IT on research is equally fundamental through the potential for change in the research process, the working methods of individual scholars, and their relationship to their discipline and to the institution. Meadows suggests caution in predicting the rate of change, because of the built-in resistance of scholars to changing their style of information handling, unless they perceive very clear benefits to make the effort worthwhile. No longer, however, are computing tools and choices only available to those in scientific research – they are available to everyone through the ubiquitous personal computer and telecommunications networks. Satellite communication and high-speed networking are loosening the boundaries of the traditional campus as they open up greater international collaboration in research. Meadows foresees an increasing diversity of formats in information transfer by researchers, with traditional and electronic forms co-existing for some time, and a much larger potential impact still to be realised in the areas of conceptual and formal communication.

New information systems and services are expensive and it is not yet clear that the new media are completely supplanting the old. In any event their use will be limited until there is more widespread awareness of the opportunities they create. There are significant economic issues to be addressed, as expensive choices need to be made, involving shifts of funding into technologies with inherently short, and shortening, investment cycles. A major player in this strategy will be the publishing industry, the main supplier of formal, external information, which has been the traditional province of libraries. Summers gives a fairly conservative view from the industry, predicting in the next five years no major shift from print on paper technology. However, he does recognise the increasing importance of, and interest in, the compact disc and sees continuing growth in the online and on-demand publishing markets.

From a library perspective, McLean explores the relevance of a user-driven model of the organisation of information systems. Perhaps surprisingly he shows that expenditure on traditional library resources, at least in the UK polytechnic sector, has been relatively stable over the last five years. However, he argues strongly that there will need to be an economic restructuring, towards the higher costs of information services, but leaves for debate in the institution who will bear that cost and what role the library will play in the acquisition, provision and transmission of new information resources.

The organisational theme is explored further by Sidgreaves who recognises early in his paper that the implications of the electronic campus cannot simply be contained in a re-definition of the roles of libraries and computing services. The opportunities offered will impact on the whole of the institution's work, and require an overall IT strategy to manage more distributed information systems. He calls for more flexibility and a clearer understanding by those involved in areas of service provision, of the changing educational processes, and their role in support of learning, teaching and research.

A recurring point of emphasis throughout the conference is the need for integrated planning and responsibility for campus IT, as a context for action. It is no longer a case of applying new technology to the traditional education and research functions of higher education: rather there is a revolution underway. If there is any doubt about it then a reading of Brown's extensive overview of trends in technology in higher education will confirm the point. He envisages that in the context of global economies and society, the internationally extended university will become a reality. He advocates a concerted and integrated effort to plan for change in higher education, with care and concern for what happens to the student participants before they come to the university and after they leave it.

The strategic planning approach is discussed by Hayes as he outlines the approach taken at UCLA to strategic planning for information resources in the research university. The process adopted for involving members of the academic staff in the definition of needs commends itself as the foundation for electronic campus developments. His overview is complemented by several case studies of UK institutions committed in their different ways to the development of the electronic campus. That the approaches taken are so varied is encouraging: that the range of institutions described is so varied confirms the relevance of the concept. All institutions need to pay attention to how IT helps them achieve the goals of higher education and how it will shape future demand and delivery, unless they wish to have an increasingly marginal role in both education and society. The proper harnessing of IT to the purposes of universities and polytechnics, coupled with the related development of creative talents of both students and academics, should ensure the continuing relevance of these institutions into the next century.

Participants at the Electronic Campus conference

Introduction to the Conference

Sir Peter Swinnerton-Dyer, *Chairman of the University Grants Committee*

One of the many starry-eyed visitors to the Soviet Union between the wars greeted the assembled press on his return to the West with the words, I have seen the future, and it works! We now know that what he saw was only one of a number of possible futures, and that it worked even less well than contemporary capitalism. I am reminded of this story whenever I hear an enthusiast for the electronic campus. That is a development suited only to a certain type of university, but it is a type which almost every British university aspires to belong to and our colleagues have invested so much rhetoric in it that we have to make it work.

The immediate consequence of the electronic campus will be an improvement in communications. Within twelve months, the Vice-Chancellor of Aston will be able to put a message into the electronic mailbox of every member of his staff – and by interrogating the system he can find out which members of the staff have read the message. There will also be improved communication between equals. But there is not much in this which is peculiar to universities: every major organisation is improving its communication in much the same way – and the automated factory shows that there is the same need to improve communications even if one dispenses with people. But a university is a special purpose organisation; what are the implications of the electronic campus for those special purposes? Two of these special purposes appear crucial in this context: that a university is a place where one learns, and that it (and particularly its library) is a repository of knowledge.

In considering learning it is useful to distinguish three kinds of topic, even though the division between them is not sharp. First, skills. For many skills, we already know how to write interactive computer programs which will do a better job of teaching than human beings can be expected to; indeed, some such programs exist already. But while one can sensibly think in terms of unit cost of teaching by human beings, writing a computer program for teaching involves a substantial basic cost but additional students cost almost nothing. Whether such a computer program is worthwhile therefore depends on student demand. In particular, one should think in terms of a national demand, rather than meeting the need within a single university.

The next group, of which mathematics is typical, consists of those subjects which are concerned with revealed truth. Here teaching is interactive only in so far as it is remedial; and remedial teaching has to be one-to-one. In a few years' time we can expect that every good lecture in such a subject will be videotaped and available in the library, so that students can replay it when they choose. (The cost of this would be small: it has nothing in common with the production of videotaped courses to Open University standards). This will raise two questions which we shall wish to evade though we will not be allowed to: why should a lecturer be paid to repeat the same lectures year after year, and why are essentially interchangeable lectures given at fifty-odd universities in Great Britain?

The third group, of which philosophy and economics are typical, consists of those subjects in which there is no such thing as absolute truth and the main object of education is to sharpen the mind by debate. This is the group of subjects which is least amenable to modern technology, and for some considerable time I do not expect its use to extend beyond information retrieval.

But there is a major obstacle to the application of up-to-date technology to learning: that is the conservatism of both academic staff and students. We are still coming to terms with the last major revolution in publishing – that associated with Gutenberg and Caxton. At the start of this decade, when I gave up teaching, many lecturers were still writing their lectures word by word on the blackboard so that each student could individually write them down; and if one distributes duplicated lecture notes, students no longer know what they are meant to do during lectures.

When I was a young academic, libraries had a fairy-tale quality. By this I mean that they contained pearls of wisdom, but to reach those pearls one had to overcome considerable obstacles – and in extreme cases even to slay dragons. Librarians nowadays seem to be younger and are certainly more helpful to users. But to balance this, another obstacle has become more serious; libraries contain far more material irrelevant to my needs than they did a generation ago. Frequently it involves less effort to rediscover something for oneself than to find it in the literature. Aids to literature retrieval are being developed and it is beginning to be accepted (at least in journal-based subjects) that retrieval will have to be based on content and not simply on bibliographic information. But there is a long way to go and in one respect a major revolution of attitude is needed.

A generation ago it could be assumed that when something was published it thereby became accessible to the scholarly world. Now, it cannot be regarded as accessible unless its existence has been recognised by an effective information retrieval system. The most important of these systems is the 'invisible college' in the particular subject; and a major advantage which it has over any more formal system is that it does not simply take accept/reject decisions but processes the material that comes into it. To computerise that last step would need advances in artificial intelligence far beyond anything one can foresee.

Nevertheless, the organisation of knowledge must involve accept/reject decisions and though it may not be a librarian's job to take those decisions, it is certainly part of a librarian's job to ensure that they are taken. Financial necessity has suppressed the magpie instinct which was so evident in an earlier generation of librarians. It is therefore worth pointing out that two of the most impressive artificial intelligence programs now operating have as their object the winnowing of a small amount of valuable information from a great mass of irrelevancies. One, of which I know only by rumour, is the program which the intelligence services use to select what is of interest from the great mass of telephone and wireless material to which they listen in daily. This program must be general-purpose but may be extremely crude; plainly one is never going to know.

The other, which is extremely special-purpose but not at all crude, operates at CERN and has look-alikes in every high energy physics laboratory. What is normally called a single experiment in such a laboratory consists in fact of a great number of collisions of particles, each collision being a separate event. Almost all these events are of no interest, since they exhibit phenomena which are already well known; it is therefore necessary to select out, in real time, the minute proportion which are of interest. One cannot afford to discard any of these because to do so would distort the statistics on which the subsequent theorising is based. One also cannot afford to retain too many uninteresting events because that would render intolerably burdensome the detailed examination of those events which are retained.

Advisedly or not, we have allowed our colleagues to make large promises on what will be gained by implementing the electronic campus; and we have been funded by the Government on the basis of those promises. Thirty years ago the same thing happened over the great expansion of the British university system.

3

On that occasion we failed to deliver the good things we had promised. This time we had better succeed.

Carlos the dealer

Professor Tom Stonier (left), Bradford University and Nigel Gardner, Economic and Social Research Council

Some no hoper's

Bringing the Electronic Campus to Reality: Opportuni Challenges in Teaching

Nigel Gardner, *Economic and Social Research Council*

Almost every day, new products and opportunities emerge within the rapidly converging technologies of computing and telecommunications. Within the last five years alone, we have witnessed unparalleled developments in process lithography and component miniaturisation, advances in storage technologies, significant refinements in programming tools and user interfaces, and sustained improvement in the design and implementation of heterogeneous and distributed networks and parallel system architectures. Campus computing has changed apace, albeit less quickly than some might wish. Some of our universities now benefit from a high bandwidth communications network, a hierarchical arrangement of computing power, and, especially at lower levels in that hierarchy, machines which offer intuitive user interfaces and the illusion of total control.

The electronic campus is, therefore, already a technical possibility. There remain a few technical wrinkles to be ironed out, but it is no overstatement to claim that these are trivial compared with the technical achievements of recent years. Indeed, some, even within senior policy formulation bodies for UK higher education, share in that optimistic vision of the future which holds that it is just a matter of time before our campuses become fully 'computerised'. It is often implicitly assumed that such rich IT environments will be inherently better educationally than our universities are now. Whilst the networked campus may conceivably confer competitive advantage, in securing and retaining the best faculty and students, there is no evidence that it automatically effects sustained improvements in the quality of teaching, learning and scholarship. Some of the more publicised US experiments in campus computing, particularly those initiated in the period 1983 to 1986, were directed by individuals who were apparently mesmerised by a vision of a silicon future, strangely oblivious to the fact that the real hurdles facing those seeking to exploit information and communications technologies in universities, as elsewhere, are ultimately not technical; the challenges in bringing the electronic campus to reality are economic, political, social, and educational in character. Successful integration of technology into higher education cannot be assured just by sinking massive resources into better, brighter software, or by facilitating a smooth transition to

5

yet another set of networking standards. Important though those issues are, they are ultimately secondary to the pervasive non-technical considerations which inhibit our successful exploitation of technology.

The recent history of educational computing in British universities exemplifies the dangers of an overly technology-oriented approach in problem delimitation and resource provision. The Nelson Report [1], published almost five years ago, reviewed the then disappointingly low level of activity in educational computing in UK universities. The report gave only a partial picture of groups and individuals active at that time in the UK, and neglected to acknowledge the very creditable contributions which UK based academics and researchers had, throughout the seventies and early eighties, made to the emerging field of IT applications in education and training. Nor indeed did the Nelson Report present any very clear vision of how or why computers might be used in teaching and learning. For all its latent technological determinism, the Nelson Report did at least precipitate a debate within the Computer Board for Universities and Research Councils (CBURC), which culminated late in 1984 with the introduction of a new special initiative designed to promote the effective use of computers in UK university teaching. With the added participation in 1985 of the University Grants Committee (UGC), the Computers in Teaching Initiative (CTI) has blossomed into a significant experiment in UK higher education. The programme retains its early aspirations to raise the issue of greater and more productive use of educational computing on personal, departmental, and institutional agendas. With its growth into a fully-fledged national initiative, the CTI acquired ancillary aims such as to evaluate more fully the educational potential of the new technology, and to enhance awareness and experience of IT among lecturers and students in all disciplines. Above all, the CTI has sought to dissect the promotional gimmickry which surrounds so much of computing. Fuller accounts of the administrative details surrounding the CTI have appeared elsewhere [2], and the initiative's regular newsletter, *The CTISS File* [3], describes the achievements of individual projects participating in the programme.

In my view, the most significant contribution of the CTI has been to highlight the organisational and institutional character of the inhibitors to success in educational computing in universities. Decisions about funding would-be participants in the programme were predicated on criteria which were in large measure technical in character. Applicants described in their proposals, at the behest of the funding agencies, details of how they would bring the latest bat-

Table 1 Landmark 'Computers in Teaching' projects
in higher education - 1988

	Project	Institution(s)	Methodology/Content
1	PERSEUS	Harvard/Boston	Text and visual database on Classical Greece
2	INTERMEDIA	Brown (IRIS)	Hypertext associations using text and graphics for literature teaching
3	THEORIA	Carnegie-Mellon	Interactive video in the teaching of ethics
4	Illinois Chemistry Project	Illinois	Interactive videodisc for introductory chemistry
5	CIText	Cambridge Glasgow Keele Birmingham York	Computer illustrated text for teaching mathematics, statistics and physics
6	DISH	Glasgow	Using databases for teaching history
7	StrathTutor	Strathclyde	Learning-by-browsing tutorial system used with bioscience students
8	Leeds Electrical Engineering Project	Leeds	Windows-based software for electrical engineering
9	MENS	Bremen	Software for teaching about non-linear systems

as lecturers begin to work with a new cadre of individuals. It poses similar threats to staff-student relations, potentially undermining the organisational legitimacy and concomitant power conferred on tutors; using computers quickly changes the lecture theatre into a laboratory, encouraging duologue and conversation rather than professorial monologue. It is parenthetically worth noting that if every student has a microcomputer we shall possibly lose that laboratory-style interaction which has so often been cited as a positive product of using computers in teaching.

Just as software needs to be reviewed, tested, and evaluated, so the broader educational impacts of using computers in teaching warrant attention. We may have far too few measures of educational outcome and quality, but there are considerably more than some of our colleagues in universities would credit. Working at the sharp end of higher education, CTI project directors have reported on the outcomes of their efforts, which they see in the classroom, the lecture theatre, and the tutorial exchange every day [10]. The problem is in quantifying achievements and collecting sufficient data to demonstrate the instructional effectiveness of new technology. The considerable literature on this topic is all too often ignored in the UK [11].

Many successful innovations, in higher education as elsewhere, have been predicated on their acceptably low up-front costs and their minimal impact on the system as a whole. The electronic campus does not come cheap, nor can we contain its pervasive impact on all aspects of our academic lives. An urgent priority must therefore be to ensure that the investments we make now are sustainable. We have seen too many initiatives which start with a big splash only to wither and die a year or two later. Sustainable investment in this context means affordable technology with pervasive consequences. A common failing has been a lack of appreciation of the very real costs in being at the forefront of technical innovation. We may all want our campuses to emulate the pioneering work of MIT, Brown, Carnegie-Mellon, Drexel, and Dartmouth – but do we really want to incur all of the learning costs and false starts experienced at those sites? All were significant experiments in campus computing, but none provides a model for sustainable investment for routine operational use of computers in teaching [12].

But perhaps the greatest challenge of all rests with those responsible for devising IT strategy in UK higher education. The problem here is that it is not entirely clear how this particular function is discharged. Universities lack the management structure necessary to address strategic issues relating to the future scale and scope of IT provision. In only a few cases, such as Aston, Southampton and Salford, is any one one individual responsible for leading debate on IT provision across the full range of campus activities. A more common model is that IT is equated with computing, and mainframe computing at that. For all the improvements and moderations in attitude of recent years the perception remains among many academics that computer centre directors and their staff are primarily concerned with satisfying the demands for research-oriented, numerically intensive computation, and they are less exercised by the more diffuse IT requirements of humanities and social science researchers, undergraduates, and others seeking simply to access IT resources as a productivity tool in their own university work (e.g. through the use of word processing and local, national, and international electronic mail). Computing strategy has for too long been regarded as something that takes place only once every few years in British universities, usually timed immediately to precede a mainframe procurement, a process which is itself dominated by a group on campus which may not be best placed to address questions of campus-wide needs and appropriate strategies for satisfying those needs.

The existing institutional structures for campus computing in British universities do not always mesh happily with the aspirations and needs of the growing number of academics seeking to use computers in their teaching. It may well be that the reform of those structures should be the first agenda item for those trying to ensure that the electronic campus of the future really does provide a wealth of opportunities in teaching and learning.

Notes and references

[1] *Report of a Working Party on Computer Facilities for Teaching in Universities*. London: Computer Board for Universities and Research Councils, 1983.

[2] Gardner, N. Integrating computers into the university curriculum. *Computers and Education*, 12(1), 1988, 23-7.

[3] *The CTISS File* appears thrice annually and is available free of charge from the Computers in Teaching Initiative Support Service, University of Bath, Claverton Down, Bath, Avon, BA2 7AY, UK.

[4] For an expansion of the issues in this paragraph refer to Kiesler, S. B. & L. S. Sproull (eds). *Computing and Change on Campus*. New York: Cambridge University Press, 1987.

[5] Aston and Bradford Universities in England are both now embarking on substantial enhancements to campus communications infrastructure. In the case of the £4 million project at Aston, the development is backed by a DTI grant under that department's Open Systems Interconnection (OSI) Awareness programme. At Bradford, support is being received from the University Grants Committee (£710 000) and from the Manpower Services Commission (£150 000).

[6] Gardner, N. No more than a tool. *The Times Higher Education Supplement*, 815, 17 June 1988.

[7] Further details on all the projects listed in Table 1 are available from the author or from the CTISS office in Bath (cf. Note 3).

[8] Details of the NCRIPTAL scheme are given in Kozma, R. B., R. L. Bangert-Downs, & J. Johnston. *The 1987 EDUCOM-NCRPITAL Higher Education Software Awards*. University of Michigan, 1987. The SRAS programme is briefly described in *The Chronicle of Higher Education*, 17 February 1988.

[9] Cartwright, G. P. & C. A. Cartwright. Software development: consideration for promotion and tenure. *Academic Computing*, Spring 1987, 14-17.

[10] I have enlarged upon this theme in Gardner, N. Advancing humanities education? Or selling our souls? In Miall, D. (ed). *Evaluating the Impact of Information Technology in the Arts and Humanities*. Bath, CTISS/CNAA, 1988, 33-41.

[11] See for example Hasselbring, T. Research on the effectiveness of computer-based instruction: a review. *International Review of Education*, 23, 1986, 313-24. Another useful reference is Johnston, J. *Electronic Learning: from Audiotape to Videodisc*. Hillside, N. J.: Lawrence Erlbaum Associates, 1987.

[12] The theme of sustainable investment and affordable technology is well developed in the latest FIPSE Technology Study Group Report, *Ivory Towers, Silicon Basements: Learner Centred Computing in Postsecondary Education*. McKinney, TX, 1988.

Higher Education and the Influence of Information Technology: Research

Professor A Jack Meadows, *Loughborough University*

Introduction

Research can be divided into a number of stages, starting with the generation of new ideas, progressing through experimentation or other kinds of testing/development, and ending with the discussion and dissemination of results. The question to be asked here is – what impact is automated information handling having on any, or all, of these stages?

In recent years, with the growth of networking, electronic interchange between academic sites has expanded rapidly. This network traffic, on analysis, proves to have been mainly in the following areas: (1) access to national computer centres; (2) resource sharing between sites; (3) software distribution; (4) multilab-site research collaboration; (5) database access; (6) human communication (mainly electronic mail). Much research activity using computers remains, of course, within the institution and does not appear in the network traffic. A study of university staff carried out a couple of years ago shows the following distribution of computer-related activity [1].

Table 1

Computer activity	% of respondents who had used a computer for this purpose
Word processing	45
Graphical display of data	38
Data analysis	36
Storing experimental data	34
Data collection	23
Searching online databases	18
Personal bibliographic index	17
Non-bibliographic database	14
Electronic mail	11

Clearly, the use of computers for a range of research purposes is already widespread (and still growing). However, before considering how this affects the various stages of research, we should look at the IT infrastructure required if most researchers' information handling needs are to be satisfied.

Workstations and networks

In the United States, discussions of the 'wired campus' are now being accompanied by discussions of the 'wired scholar'. The latter sounds rather more uncomfortable than the former, but the coupling of the two phrases reflects the two basic elements in current discussions of researchers' needs – workstations for individual scholars and networks to link them together.

A workstation, as envisaged in these discussions, is essentially a computer terminal which integrates a wide range of activities. It can store and analyse experimental data, send messages to colleagues, handle text, acquire journal articles in electronic form and so on. Equipment with these capabilities is expensive; so the word 'workstation' is often applied to terminals which can only provide a restricted range of these facilities. If researchers' needs are to be properly met, the trend must be in the opposite direction, i.e. to expand the facilities available even on what are now regarded as genuine workstations. The reason is that all analyses of researchers' activities demonstrate not only the range, but also the volume of information that must be handled. Discussions in the United States now revolve round the possibility of producing a 'scholar's workstation' (a phrase that seems to have originated early in the 1980s at Brown University). This goal has been described as the requirement to produce a '3-M' machine: that is, a workstation with a memory of one million bytes, a display screen of one million pixels, and an operating speed of one million instructions per second. Obviously, if such a workstation is to communicate with others efficiently, it must have access to a network which can handle millions of bits of information per second. This latter requirement is easier to arrange within single institutions, using local area networks (LANs) than between institutions, using wide area networks (WANs). For international traffic the problems are considerably larger, though some high-volume flow of research information is being handled by satellites.

In principle, efficient workstations connected by efficient networks provide an adequate infrastructure for all the basic information handling needs of researchers. In practice, other problems have to be solved. An obvious one is interfacing between systems and networks. In addition, workstations must be connected to other facilities – from mainframes to printers. The question of how these various linked elements are to be juggled in order to provide an optimum service is likely to form a continuing problem. As all this will suggest, very few researchers currently have access to anything like the optimum information handling facilities. The question, at present, is what can be done with the facilities available.

Researchers and information handling

The different stages of any research project can be analysed in terms of the information and communication activities they imply. For example, conversation with colleagues often figures largely when an experiment is being set up, whilst communication with journals becomes essential at the dissemination stage. Conversation, telephone calls and similar exchanges of information are usually referred to as 'informal' communication. This distinguishes them from information in journals, books, or other long-term storage media, which represents 'formal' communication. In addition, there is the information stored and created in the mind of the researcher, which can be described as 'conceptual'. The key question then is how IT can aid these three types of information handling – conceptual, informal and formal.

One basic factor deserves emphasis. Researchers have a built-in resistance to changing their style of information handling. Any new alternative must offer very clear benefits in order to be adopted. This resistance derives from a number of factors. One is that researchers have expended considerable effort and time in developing their methods of information acquisition and handling. Their interest is in the information rather than the process of acquisition; so they prefer to keep the 'information capital' they have built up, rather than spend time on learning new techniques. What is true of the individual researcher is also true of the research community. For example, each research community has developed its own methods of vetting to ensure that only material of acceptable quality is published. It will look suspiciously at any approach to communicating research that appears to subvert this aim. Finally, of course, any new communication medium must be able to compete with existing media in terms of physical acceptability to the researcher. This does not mean that new information handling techniques must be superior across the board to older techniques. For example, retrieval of information at a terminal is geographically restricted, whereas a printed journal can be read anywhere. But this disadvantage may be cancelled

15

out if speed of retrieval or comprehensive coverage are important. So there can be a trade-off for new media in terms of advantages and disadvantages.

Conceptual information handling

Computer aids to conceptual information handling by researchers are very limited at present. There are various software packages available for putting ideas into a logical sequence and interconnecting them. But attempts to mimic human thinking and so help in the generation of new concepts are still at an early stage. Current interest centres on two activities: (1) the creation of 'ideas' leading to the development of new research queries; (2) determination of the research strategies that might be used to investigate these queries. Expert systems are complementary to this work in the sense that they are concerned with answering queries rather than posing them. Some work on research strategy uses a similar approach to expert system techniques in that it relies on sampling opinions from a population of experienced researchers. At the moment, the impact of this work on researchers is negligible, but it looks set to receive more emphasis in the 1990s.

Acquisition of information

The stimulation of new ideas comes, in part, from the inflow of information to the researcher via both formal and informal communication channels. This inflow is already being affected by IT. The growth in volume of research publications has been paralleled by an increased awareness on the part of researchers of their need to keep up with the information as it appears. Table 2 illustrates this point [2]. This enhanced awareness of information is accompanied by an increased willingness to use electronic means of access.

There are already signs that the availability of information via computer may provide researchers with more flexible access. For example, online public access catalogues (OPACs) are now becoming available in higher education. Preliminary analysis of the use of OPACs suggests that scholars can now acquire information in a way more appropriate for their subject. For example, researchers in science and technology clearly find subject headings provide the most useful means of access, whereas their counterparts in arts and social science still tend to prefer the traditional entry points of author or title. It should be added that OPACs also permit researchers' use of information to be monitored, so allowing the provision of the information, itself, to be modified and made

Table 2

Information-seeking activity	% of researchers involved	
	1962	1985
Follow up references cited in relevant papers	80	96
Keep up with literature by reading current publications	77	95
Search the subject or author indexes of abstract journals	55	68
Use a personal index or other personal record	47	54
Use a library index or catalogue	10	31

more cost-efficient.

Another example of combining speed and flexibility in retrieval is the rapidly growing use of hypertext (or, more generally, hypermedia). Here a particular trend of importance to researchers relates to electronic full-text versions of journal articles. Using hypertext, the researcher can pull up different sections of the article onto the screen simultaneously. For example, whenever the main text makes a citation to another work, the list of references can be pulled up for consultation. It is then possible, in principle, to pull up the article cited in the references to see whether it is relevant to the reader's needs. At present, these possibilities are only in the formative stage, since a good deal of pre-planning is necessary to allow such access. The flexibility of this approach may eventually apply not only to what additional information is pulled up, but also to the form in which it is presented. For example, a reader might be able to choose between having data presented via a verbal description, or tabulated, or in graphic form.

New developments, such as hypertext, are also beginning to meet one of the long-standing complaints against electronic information handling – that it removes the ability to browse. Many ideas are picked up from unexpected sources – from books on library shelves adjacent to the actual book being sought, from items in newspapers, and so on. Hitherto, electronic information handling gave little opportunity for this kind of spin-off, but more flexible modes of accessing are beginning to change this position.

Analysis of information

The use of computers to analyse experimental data or develop theoretical models requires little comment, since this has been a major application of computers from the very early days. But some current developments involving automated information handling are worth remarking. The first point is that computer usage is now commonplace in all areas of research, not just in science and technology. This is illustrated by the figures in Table 3 for British universities [1]. In fact, it makes sense to suppose that future researchers in the humanities may make more use of computers than many scientists. Over a wide range of subjects, especially in languages and history, much research is done on texts. This can now often be handled more satisfactorily on computer than on paper. The classicists, for example, are well advanced on a programme of digitising all classical texts.

Table 3

Activity	% using computer in each subject area		
	Science	Social Science	Arts
Word processing	58	63	62
Data analysis	55	53	25
Storage of data	42	48	48
Data collection	40	17	24
Searching online databases	28	15	22
Personal bibliographic databases	18	30	26

A second point concerns the interactive use of computers in experimentation. Use of equipment at a distant site by remote control is on the increase. It can be accompanied by reduction of the data in real time to assess what further observations need to be made. In some cases, automatic monitoring of conditions is included, e.g. of animal houses in biomedical experiments. The overall effect is that computers are no longer used simply as the concluding stage of an experimental investigation: they are often now involved throughout.

Informal communication

One activity that continues through all the stages of research is discussions with colleagues, reading of newsletters, etc. Various IT facilities – electronic mail, bulletin boards, computer conferencing, etc. – are having an impact on these activities. Electronic bulletin boards are still at the initial growth stage in the UK, but are already being used for a wide range of information, such as forthcoming meetings, new and completed research projects, grants awarded, notes, queries and comments. The information they contain is being supplemented by more permanent databases, e.g. ones collecting and collating information on research in progress.

Electronic messaging is already commonplace in UK higher education. Messaging fills a gap between traditional letters and telephone calls. It is much faster than the former, but does not require real-time contact with a colleague like the latter. This reflects an important aspect of informal 'discussion' using IT: it typically supplements existing communication channels rather than replacing them. Recent studies suggest that over half of computer-mediated communications would not have taken place in the absence of the computer. In other words, the improvement of IT-based communication results in a considerable increase not merely in the amount of information in circulation, but in the number and variety of messages transmitted.

By no means all IT communication opportunities are used simply because they are there. An example is computer conferencing. Usage of this is still small, and its increase may depend on the realisation that computer conferencing is not a replacement for ordinary conferences, but, again, a supplementary form of communication. Networks cannot reproduce all the nuances of face-to-face contact; in any case, the ethos of most research communities requires that members get together at intervals.

Formal communication

IT is already providing a significant extension of informal communication. Its role in formal communication has so far been much more limited. This is because formal communication is both much more standardised and carries more weight. For example, the research community is organised to bestow recognition in terms of contributions to the published literature. This makes it much more difficult to move away from the established medium of print-on-paper. In addition, there are major problems of electronic access, especially internationally. Hence, although an electronic journal has been tried with some success on an experimental basis, further development in that direction is likely to be slow compared with the growth of informal electronic communication.

One exception to this general statement occurs when electronic media offer major improvements for the transfer of information – for example, where large quantities of data need to be made available, or extensive graphics must be provided. Even so, multi-media transfer is likely to be the preferred option. For example, a discussion printed in hard copy might be accompanied by a compact disc. This is an extension of the use of microform by some publishers to provide a data back-up to journal articles.

IT is already being extensively used by scholarly publishers as part of their production of printed journals and books. An example is computer-aided refereeing, where editors use a computer database to assist in selecting and contacting referees for journal articles. More obviously, there is now a strong move towards accepting material for publication in machine-readable form. Word-processing packages are becoming increasingly sophisticated, and software is now on the market to support group writing of articles between researchers situated at different sites. One of the hold-ups in preparation of articles and reports has been the relatively high proportion of researchers in the UK (more in science and technology than the humanities) who lack typing skills. By the end of the century, voice input may have developed to the point where it can be used for the production of first drafts. (This development will obviously be of wider importance than just the production of research articles.)

Cost implications

The computerisation of research activity clearly has wide-ranging consequences for the organisation of a campus. Perhaps the most important of these is the question of cost. Though both workstations and network access will undoubtedly become cheaper, the cost of producing a 'wired scholar' will remain appreciable, not least because the rapid turnover of state-of-the-art hardware and software is set to continue.

There are other less obvious problems. For example, many researchers do some of their work at home, especially those parts which entail reading or writing. Hence, there will be a call for the researcher's home to be linked to the workplace. If such home-based activities increase, what are the implications for the use of central facilities, such as the library? Many information producers have looked at the market in the light of currently changing circumstances, and have decided they should aim their pricing at end-users, rather than institutions. Again, what effect will this have on use of funding? In any case, the growth of different complementary channels of communication presumably means that the institution's total expenditure on communication will rise.

Summary

The trend in the 1980s has been for IT to become used for research in all disciplines. The 1990s will see a majority of all researchers in higher education involved in several different types of automated information handling. These new forms of information handling are as likely to supplement traditional means of communication as to replace them. Hence, information transfer by researchers will not only continue to increase in volume, but will also continue to diversify in form. The emphasis so far has been mainly on informal communication. Though developments in automation at both the conceptual and formal communication levels are progressing, their impact on research is, as yet, less evident.

References

[1] Heeks, R. *Computerisation in Academic Departments: a Survey of Current Practice*. London: Taylor Graham, 1987.

[2] Martyn, J. *Literature Searching Habits and Attitudes of Research Scientists*. London: British Library Research and Development Department (British Library Research Paper 14), 1987.

'Brushstrokes in Flight': A Strategic Overview of Trends in Technology in Higher Education

Rowland C W Brown, *OCLC Online Computer Center, Inc.*

My title, 'Brushstrokes in Flight', will be obscure to those of you who know nothing of Columbus, Ohio, and I suspect that proportion approaches 100%. It is an allusion to a sculpture by the American artist Roy Lichtenstein that was commissioned by the City of Columbus and is in front of the Columbus air terminal. It is a fifteen-foot high column representing the artist's 'brush strokes' of different colors, zigging and zagging somewhat but moving steadily upward.

The work has been controversial, some revering it as a powerful work of art, others reviling it as a piece of modernistic claptrap. I am among its admirers. I find it not only a very powerful work, but also one of great variety, imagination, elan, sweep, and above all, energy, and that is why it is relevant to my talk today, for the qualities and characteristics of 'Brushstrokes' are also qualities and characteristics of the field of information technology. IT is relentlessly dynamic and almost infinitely varied, and its very dynamism and variety pose exciting challenges and opportunities to those of us who are immersed in it.

My task, however, is not to pursue the metaphor but to turn to the more mundane – but no less fanciful – field of IT.

As I tried to develop a cogent and concise 'strategic overview' of trends in IT, I found it difficult to know where to begin. It might be expected that a 'strategic overview' of information trends in higher education would build upon the strategic issues that appeared to me to arise from the other papers prepared for this conference. However, as I have not had the opportunity at this time to read or hear my fellow participants' observations, I will have to defer this to my oral presentation. This leaves a difficult task. I certainly want to avoid a rambling discourse on what the characteristics and needs of higher education will be in the future, the magnitude of the IT revolution and its impact on those needs, and the strategic decisions and directions that need to be taken in response to these trends. That is, after all, the purpose of this entire conference. I trust, therefore, that you will indulge me in some rather sweeping generalisations about both higher education and the technology we are addressing. I will then focus on some trends and issues that I believe call for institutional, inter-institutional and national, strategic responses. At an OCLC-sponsored conference on the campus of the future, Maurice Glicksman, Provost of Brown University, stated that IT will have a profound impact on the three principal goals of higher education: (1) the creation of new knowledge; (2) the communication of knowledge; and (3) the conservation of knowledge. I agree with that assessment. Fortunately, others are focusing their considerable experience and insights on the influence of these technology trends on teaching and research. My colleague from the United States, Bob Hayes, is uniquely qualified to reflect on the increasing and varied information resources that make up the environment of higher education today and that will influence that environment in the future. I will touch on these and other areas, but only to such a degree as will support my conclusions regarding strategic implications. Thus, I may overlap to some extent with other papers, as I suspect our conference organisers anticipated.

At the outset there are two hurdles that confront me. The first is the necessity to make some assumptions on what higher education will be like in the future as the result of factors other than technology. I want to address this before I offer you some thoughts on how this vision might be further changed by technology. The second is the difficulty of speaking from experience gained primarily in the United States and superimposing the lessons of that experience on an environment, conditions and practices that, as I am increasingly cognisant, are quite different in the United Kingdom. Let me first touch briefly on this latter issue, because I believe it may introduce a perspective that will help you to place some of my views in the perspective of your experience in the United Kingdom.

In the United States we have a combination of publicly funded education – the predominant mode – and privately financed higher education with relatively autonomous governance, policy development and financing. This combination demands strategic overviews that are different from those that might be meaningful here. Also, when we in the United States speak of government direction and financing, we focus more at the state level than the national level. Thus, given the different economic conditions prevailing throughout the fifty states, the diverse state policies and structures of governance, there is significant state and even institutional autonomy, with, as one might expect, equally significant differences. In the United Kingdom, centralisation of the funding of higher education at the national level demands strategic considerations that are quite different, and I suspect that this national level involvement carries with it political considerations that an observer from abroad finds difficult to appraise. Moreover, there appear to be many important factors in the US that are less important in addressing strategic issues in the United Kingdom. In the United States, the roles of foundations, national endowments, corporate largesse and partnerships, and alumni support are significant in funding higher education, and these are heavily influenced by national and state tax policies designed to encourage private support. Such differences, together with the severe financial constraints that impede the allocation of certain types of funding, appear to present higher education in the United Kingdom with different, and I suspect, far more difficult current issues in dealing with the impact of IT than those generally confronting institutions in the US. I make these observations at the outset because the strategic overview of the roles and benefits of technology in an environment of declining resources frequently differs markedly from that in an environment of even modest expansion.

While I assume that we all approach this conference on campus information strategies with some common understanding of what we mean by 'information technology' and the trends in that technology, it would seem appropriate to make some prefatory remarks regarding our assumptions about technology. We recognise the driving force of the exponential advances in power, speed, size, and cost of 'computers', but it is the combination of computation and information processing characteristics that creates the broad implications that technology has for higher education. Moreover, while it is common to speak of it as the combination of computer and communications technologies, IT is really the confluence of many related and frequently combined technologies, all of which are changing at bewildering speeds. This is what makes the possible impact of technology on higher education so revolutionary, or as one educational administrator has described it so 'convulsive'. To make this point, I have attached a chart that we use at OCLC in tracking our technology assessment overview (Figure 1).

These trends can perhaps be summarised in the following manner:

- The speed of processing is increasing at an incredible rate. At the same time, hardware is decreasing in size, cost, and power requirements, and in most cases special environmental conditions are being eliminated. Concurrently, processing is moving towards more powerful computers whose capabilities approach those of the human brain and towards miniaturisation that will empower the individual with a scholarly workstation or a powerful portable processor at a level previously achieved only by very large and costly systems.

- The density and random accessibility of mass storage are increasing, while costs are diminishing. Again we find concurrent trends in two directions. One enables the magnitude of centrally stored data to grow to a point where limits of size are no longer significant. At the same time through distributable high-density storage in magnetic and optical modes, and combinations of these, a range of capabilities that would previously have resided only on a very large centralised system is now available to the campus, even to the departmental level and the individually accessed workstation. These will provide the individual user with significant, convenient and cost-effective access to print, graphic and audio information.

- There is steadily increasing sophistication of workstation software and user interfaces: screens with windows and icons; imaging, copying, optical scanning and character recognition; transmitting, formatting and printing of images with improved definition and color, and capabilities for enlargement and manipulation. And, of course, we are witnessing the emergence of printing or publishing on demand from digitised information warehouses and desk-top publishing systems.

- Improvements in capacity, compression techniques, and transmission prices are making communication costs relatively independent of distance and capable of combining print, graphics and sound. This will approach the convenience and the quality we have come to associate with quality publishing, and it will lead to new and exciting mixed media modes that we have never experienced in higher education.

I could go on in this vein in discussing communication protocols, software, applications, etc., but let me conclude this necessarily superficial overview of technological trends with two observations: one is that there is a need, because of the complexity and rapid change of these technologies, first to broaden technological scanning and assessment in higher education and, second, to devise an effective method of communicating to our potential users the possibilities technology offers. These activities must then become strategic planning and operating components at both the campus level and the inter-institutional and national levels. I will refer to this again in my summary.

	1970	1980	1990	2000
Processor Technologies	Mainframe Minis	Micros Fault Tolerant Supermicros Commercial Database Machines Symbolic Processors (LISP Machines) Specialized Text-Search Processors	Highly Parallel Processors Transputer	5th Generation(Non-Traditional Arch.) Optical Computers
Mass Storage Technologies	Magnetic Tape/Disk Floppy Disk	Winchester Disk Video Disk Optical Disk Optical Film Optical Card	Digital Audio Tape (DAT) Erasable Optical Digital Paper	Photon-Coated Materials (1)
Person Machine Interface	Menu/Command 'User Friendly'	Icons Pull down Menus	Common Command Language Specialised Expert Systems Some Natural Language	
Input	Keyboard Joysticks Light Pen Touch Screen Mouse	OCR Some Voice/Input High Resolution Scanners	Intelligent OCR Larger Vocabulary Voice Input/ (Speaker Dependent) Large Vocabulary Voice Input/ (Speaker Independent)	
Output	Monochrome Alpha Displays Low Resolution Graphics Color	Windowing High Resolution Graphics Voice Laser Printers Character LCD	Personal copiers/Printers Portable High Resolution Reflection Monitor (2) Hologram/Output	
Workstations	Intelligent Terminals Stand Alone Processors		CAD/CAM Workstations Personal Super Computers Personal Computer Workstations LISP Machines	Intelligent Information Appliances

Figure 1 — Developing Technologies

	1970	1980	1990	2000
Software	Specialized Modular Development Design; Structured Design; Programming Development tools; Software Engineering	Development Environments	Application Generators; Very High Level Languages	Integrated CASE Tools (3)
Telecommunications	Terrestrial (Twisted Pairs, COAX, Microwave); Satellite; Packet Networks	Local Area Networks; Fiber Optics; Divestiture	Bypass; Cellular; ISDN; Metropolitan Area Networks	Packet Radio; Space Platform
Applications	Algorithm-IC (Batch/Some Interactive)	Some Heuristics; Intelligent Networking	Some Expert Systems; Knowledge-based Programs; Machine Translation; Hypermedia-based Systems	Process of Non-Text for Retrieval

(1) New material/optical technique promising 1,000 times storage density of CD-ROM.
(2) Eyeglass-mounted reflection monitor like jet pilot's heads-up display.
(3) Semi-automated software generation from analysis through coding/testing.

Figure 1 Developing Technologies

My second observation, which is probably subject to greater challenge, is that within the next twenty years – a single generation – these technologies will provide us with new levels of access, manipulation, representation, simulation, computation, communication, storage and preservation which will support virtually any program of research, communication, teaching and learning that is currently identified or desired but has up to now been technologically impossible. Moreover, these technologies will enable us, I fear, to accomplish a great deal more than our conceptual ability will demand. Since most of us are trapped in our conceptual thinking and practices by the past and present, we may find it difficult to imagine how we can apply these technologies to tasks radically different from those we perform today. New technology is customarily used at first to replace older technology and is applied to existing practices, enabling us merely to do the same thing differently. Most of the applications on our campus, such as the library and administrative support services, fall in this category. Only in the second phase do we begin to apply the technology to genuinely new tasks or approaches made possible by the new technologies. Finally, in the later stages of the new technology, we begin to witness the societal changes which flow from the full implementation of those technologies, which themselves bring yet other new and difficult-to-forecast technological applications. Certainly the changes wrought by the automobile, the jumbo jet, and satellite transmission of television are examples of technologies which have changed the way we live, work, entertain ourselves, and look at the world. Similar sweeping changes will flow, but to an even greater degree from the impact of the combined information technologies we are now contemplating.

We should acknowledge, however, that higher education for the most part, except in certain areas of research, primarily in the hard sciences, is relatively slow to adopt new technologies. As one educator in the computer field wryly noted, it took thirty years for the overhead projector to move from the bowling alley to the classroom in the United States.

But, having said that, there can be little doubt that these technologies will have a profound impact on higher education in ways that are difficult to predict at this early stage of the development cycle.

Higher education in the United States is predicated, as Professor Francis Fisher at Harvard University has written, on a technology of printed material, classrooms and poor education or preparation at our elementary and secondary levels

[1]. The new technologies have the potential, but by no means the certainty, of changing all this. As Fisher conjectures, 'If learning becomes electronic and the schools do a much better job of teaching, institutions of higher education will be changed profoundly, regardless of the extent to which they themselves use the new technology.'[2]

Before we can realise the sweeping promise of the benefits of technology, however, we must resolve a whole series of limitations and issues that are not technological in nature. Here I am reminded of a recent remark of Dr Ohno, a quantum chemistry professor in the Faculty of Science, and Director of the University Library at Hokkaido University in Japan, who described his situation, with both excitement and humor, as a 'Time of Hope and a Pack of Problems'.

Which brings me to the central theme of this paper – the strategic issues we face in implementing technological solutions to our 'pack of problems'. To begin with, there are many factors that come into play as we try to implement new technologies in higher education. These would include the impact on or of the following:

- Our limited conceptual capability to anticipate the changes that are likely in our environment as a result of new technologies.

- Inertia of both individuals and institutions.

- The organisation, which can either facilitate or throw up barriers.

- Resources, a scarcity of which can impede or even preclude the adoption of new technologies.

- Standards in operating systems, communication protocols, interfaces, computing language, SGML, etc. (They must be adopted in higher education, and once adopted, adhered to, if we are to make cost-effective and widespread use of the new technologies on the campus, as well as on inter-institutional, national and international bases.)

- Conflicts resulting from traditional academic, teaching and publishing structures and practices and the necessity to recognise new modes of economic and professional reward in an increasingly non-print environment; and published information overload and its increasingly reduced use.

- Insufficient knowledge of how we learn and how computer technologies can effectively be used in the cognitive process.

- The complexity and cost of software development and maintenance.

- The challenges for faculty, administration, publishers and others in coping with the rapid obsolescence of constantly changing hardware and software.

Before I address these in the context of a strategic overview for higher education, let me draw your attention to some related issues that challenge us. As we consider the combined potential of the technological trends we have discussed, we cannot fail to be struck by some paradoxes. For example: these technologies both force and encourage us to centralise costly research facilities and in-depth information resources and collection and sharing information resources; at the same time, they both push and pull us to decentralise operations, distribute processing and databases and empower the campus, the department and even the individual user through academic networking on a national and international scale. Indeed, the communication structure being designed for the campus and among institutions is intended to facilitate both directions simultaneously.

Here is another paradox: these twin paths of development (i.e. centralising v. decentralising) are likely to result in (1) very capital-intensive centres of research, testing and computation, with their attendant support structures, maintenance costs and the fierce competition among institutions for resources, grants and the world's brightest and finest researchers, and/or (2) the possibility of minimising reliance on a particular geographic location or institution for resources and maximising opportunities for participation in collaborative research. The effect of both is to encourage research and learning centres but still to enable both research and learning to be carried out on a very decentralised basis, with individual scholars and researchers, at least in certain fields, being less dependent upon any particular institution.

To look at it from another angle, these technologies can be perceived as not only enriching and expanding our vision, our scope of activity and our productivity, but also as one of the principal techniques for maintaining current objectives and programmes despite substantial reductions in overall financial resources. It is understandable, therefore, that faculty and researchers have feelings of ambivalence towards the implications of these technologies. Administrators are similarly torn between anticipating the increased strain on resources that the introduction of the new technologies will have on already tight budgets and the promise that they provide for improved productivity, and reduction of redundant efforts and resources.

These technologies also have the potential to narrow the gap between the resource-rich and the resource-poor. Yet at the same time, because of the equation of information with economic power, the gap between rich and poor can be widened still further at local, national and global levels because of uneven access to these emerging technologies, particularly in their early and more costly stages. One need only look at the history of our industrial revolution to visualise the inherent conflict in the present rapidly changing scene. This conflict poses difficult policy issues for administrators at the local and national levels. It is not that unequal access is new; indeed, it has been a characteristic of higher education from the beginning. It is, rather, the potential for these new technologies both to ameliorate and exacerbate that adds to the dilemma.

In assessing the strategic implications of IT for higher education, I have assumed certain generally acknowledged demographic trends; the continued growth and proliferation of knowledge, disciplines and fields of inquiry; and the consequent explosive growth in publication. I also assume a trend toward more formal continuing education as the changes wrought by this new environment cause those in the work force to shift jobs and careers more frequently and enable many individuals to extend their institutionally supported education to a more natural life-long pursuit in an increasingly ageing population. Those institutions of higher education that provide life-long learning and develop supportive service relationships with their graduates that go beyond traditional requests for gifts will have unique advantages. With the continuing flow of students from throughout the world seeking higher education outside their own country, particularly graduate study and post-doctoral work in the United States, Canada and the United Kingdom, enrolments will continue to be increasingly multi-national in nature, and English will increasingly be the second language of a significant portion of certain segments of the student body and certain post-degree professional and instructional staff. As education and research reflect the growing global nature of our economies and societies, more institutions of higher education will affiliate with programmes abroad, enter into joint arrangements, or embark on ambitious international university structures. The internationally extended university will be a reality.

31

There is another dimension to this. I believe that for the first time in our history of education in the United Kingdom, the United States and Canada, we are gradually beginning to widen our awareness and broaden our core general education to address cultures, history, thought and values beyond those emanating from our Western European and Roman, Greek, Judaic and Christian roots. Even as North America gets ready to celebrate the 'discovery' voyages of Columbus, it is increasingly apparent that we are celebrating awareness rather than discovery, and prior discoveries and ancient links between Asian civilisation and the western hemisphere are receiving increasing attention. Similarly, I was struck by the fact that as Australia celebrates the 200th anniversary of English settlement, that nation is becoming increasingly sensitive to, and proud of, an aboriginal culture which has survived for 25 000 to 50 000 years. As institutions of higher learning in other parts of the globe, with very different traditions in education and curricula face the same intrusion of thought, experience and values from abroad, it will be difficult to ascertain what should constitute a 'core' education for our citizenry. Will our concepts of the 'classics' and classical studies begin to broaden? This is already the subject of hot political and educational debate in certain quarters in the United States. Surely our global information technologies will accelerate this phenomenon, as our already broadened global awareness in image and sound begin to be matched in written expression.

As we focus on higher education, we must take into account some factors that the new information technologies will either ameliorate or exacerbate. Let me cite a few examples:

- Some savants estimate that knowledge doubles every sixteen years, and at twice that rate in some fields. Knowledge will continue to explode, and with this explosion will come a proliferation of disciplines and publication, a potential for significant redundancy in research, and a need for interdisciplinary research.

- Many activities now identified by a location – this university or that research centre – will become less place-dependent. More important will be communities of peers at many geographic locations. Their interactions, sometimes across vast distances, will be facilitated through the libraries, computers and research systems to which they will have access.

- Identity with or loyalty to scholarly peers and field of scholarship and research will be more important to scholars than institutional commitment.

- Distance, both in time and in kilometres, will become less critical, less dividing.

- Language barriers will become less formidable to us as English increasingly becomes the language for international electronic information and control systems as well as in certain areas of scientific reporting. But as publications, particularly technical, increase in non-English languages such as Japanese, and with limited translation capabilities on our campuses and in business and government, greater attention will be given to coordinated or national efforts at translation and sophisticated machine translation capabilities in a competitive awareness effort.

- There is apt to be a greater blurring of the roles of the private and public sectors in both education and research. Certainly business is seeking and taking a bigger direct role in education.

- Institutions of higher education and certain agencies of government upon whom education depends will more and more be driven to cost recovery and even to generating profits in furnishing services or exploiting the fruits of their research. Many faculty members are becoming increasingly entrepreneurial. If a new university were formed today, it would be interesting to see if a different model would be followed. Perhaps Bond University in Australia will prove to be an interesting study.

- There will be increasing resort to national efforts in academic networking and resource sharing.

- Tension between publishers and educational institutions and their faculties will grow, both from the impact of the new information technologies on intellectual property rights and from the rapid rise in journal subscription prices and proliferation of titles. This, in turn, is likely to result in more joint ventures among the members of the scholarly community, higher education, government and publishers; exploration of new document delivery services and journal publications; and the development of new electronic publishing and distribution services like EIDOS and ADONIS.

As other papers to be presented at this conference will undoubtedly demonstrate in detail, IT is having a revolutionary impact on the conduct of research, primarily in certain scientific fields. But, this impact is quickly spreading to all areas of scholarship and research, from high energy physics to archaeology and anthropology, from genetics to psychology and the behavioural sciences, to the classics, music and philosophy. Improved productivity, communication with unseen colleagues, remote access and control of experimental equipment, and avoidance of redundant work which might otherwise result from the proliferation of disciplines are opportunities for application.

As equipment and support services required to conduct research attract outstanding researchers to ones campus grow to staggering proportions, and as government funding on campus, particularly from defence and other nationally directed programmes, grows, it will be a challenge for education administrators to determine how the new information technologies can be used to share or equalise the impact of this new phenomenon of capital-intensive research and the growing size of research teams.

Others at this conference will be focusing their efforts on the impact of these information technologies on teaching, and I suspect, learning as well. From the perspective of strategic consideration, allow me a few general observations. These new technologies offer exciting possibilities in improving our teaching methods, and freeing us even more from the traditional confines of time and space. Similarly, as we learn more about how we learn, these technologies should help us. But this will not happen, in my judgment, unless there is a much more concerted allocation of resources within the higher education community to these ends. It must become part of the strategic directions of educational leadership.

There has been little evidence to date that technology has played a significant role either in improved learning or teaching. But that is not surprising in that most of the barriers to the introduction and application of the previously described new technologies are particularly applicable in this area. Despite a few outstanding examples to the contrary, most efforts at courseware or educational software have not been particularly noteworthy. Moreover, there is an absence of an effective means of communicating about such software. OCLC and EDUCOM in the United States are about to undertake a pilot project which will provide online access to existing educational software, where it is being used, its acceptance, and the conditions under which it can be obtained and used.

The biggest problem will be to bring the faculty into the process of using these technologies. An in-depth knowledge of the potential and the application of such tools as computer-assisted simulation, holographic representation and mixed media presentation is essential. Such understanding will prove difficult for those faculty who have traditionally viewed 'technology' as remote or threatening.

Exposure to the implication of those technologies, sufficient hands-on training and technical staff support will be imperative. To master these tools will require an investment on the part of the user, taking time away from the ever more taxing task of mastering one's subject knowledge as well as related disciplines. We are unaccustomed to this as most of our tool learning was gained in our youth. One only has to see how older practitioners who did not become proficient in what is now referred to as 'keying', formerly 'typing', find themselves less comfortable with the desk-top or lap computer than their younger counterparts who depend upon them in every phase of their work, including exam-taking. New alternative entry and manipulation methods will help.

The fact is that the new technologies will not have a broad impact on our curricula, our teaching, and our research until they become so imbedded in what we do that we don't notice it. Because we are talking about tools and habits rather than accumulated knowledge, it may turn out to be a generational phenomenon.

In a recent survey conducted by the US Congress Office of Technology Assessment, there was general consensus that significant improvement in learning will be achieved in the next fifteen to twenty years if a major effort is made to implement these information technologies into the process.

Although my remarks are primarily directed to the broad components of higher education, I hope you will allow me a few observations about one specific component, the library.

Let me quote from a presentation by John Haeger, an officer of the Research Libraries Group, at a recent conference we participated in with representatives of both US and Japanese library leaders. He pointed to the remarkable changes that had come to pass in just the past decade in how we provide access to the user and how data or information can be manipulated and personalised [3]:

In 1978, our [the library] world was firmly bibliocentric. We were concerned about library problems: acquisitions, processing and preservation. We nurtured a fuzzy vision of so-called public access terminals hidden amidst card catalogs – ultimately replacing them – but we worried about the number of terminals we would need to provide and the size of the CPU to support them. The computer revolution...changed all that...a world of individual scholar workstations emerged: workstations equipped with powerful CPUs, graphics and windowing; running word processing, database, spreadsheet and desktop-publishing software; connected to university-based local area networks and gatewayed to one or more bibliographic utilities; able to access the utilities' databases to create interlibrary loan requests and electronic mail and to download data for subsequent manipulation in the workstation; able to integrate the imported data with non-bibliographic data (full text, statistics, and image) from other sources in hypertext.

The technology is all there. We at OCLC, for example, are either already providing support for such services to libraries, their institutions and users, or are developing it. Searching capabilities, in both online or CD-ROM modes, of bibliographic and full text databases are growing monthly. We expect, in our EIDOS services, to provide searching of title pages, tables of contents and back-of-the-book indexes of recent publications in selected disciplines to supplement the online public access library catalog. This will be supplemented with search access to the content or full text and the capability to print out selected portions of both text and graphics to the extent that this proves to be economically feasible and that licensing rights from collaborative publishers can be obtained. 'Campus information systems' will soon replace or wrap themselves around the earlier generation of automated library systems, and OCLC's joint efforts with Carnegie-Mellon University, the Mercury Project, is an example of an effort directed to a broad-based university system to provide all the features described by Haeger and a good deal more.

But as universities assess the future of libraries and their changing role on the campus, note should be taken that academic and research libraries face the combined challenge of (1) collection and storage of growing amounts of print information; (2) the necessity, particularly in this transition era, of acquiring print, microform and electronic versions of similar or identical materials; (3)

providing their patrons increased access to online information resources that introduce a use cost not associated with their traditional print materials; (4) the heavy costs of preservation of deteriorating print materials; and (5) the need to automate both technical services and public services in the broad scope previously described and to convert to electronic form a backlog of large older collections if they are to be accessed in their online environment. This will increasingly place a very heavy financial strain on libraries. Traditional institutional budgeting and allocation formulas will not allow libraries to provide the level of support the scholarly and research communities will demand. University administrations will have to reassess the new costs of information access, storage, and preservation and wrestle with the difficult issues of how the costs will be borne.

The library's role on the campus must be reassessed. It must recognise that it has a new part to play – or that it must carry out its mission in new ways. As I have already noted, changes in IT will mean that users will not necessarily need or wish to be within the library's walls to access its contents, nor will they want to be confined to the information resources that are physically within those walls. 'Access' is and will be the buzzword, and linking with other libraries and with national and international databases, bibliographic and other, will identify the existence and location of material. Efficient, electronically driven interlibrary lending augmented by electronic document delivery will support increased resource-sharing.

We have traditionally sought information from many sources, particularly from our colleagues and peers and from our own private treasuries. New technologies now allow us to seek and collect massive quantities of information in electronic format within the university but without the knowledge, control or budgetary support of the library. These collections of information are rarely gathered with an eye toward universal access and are often unknown to anyone but the person or persons collecting them. This raises serious issues, not just for the information manager but for other scholars who could benefit from access to the information.

Given the likely financial restraints, librarians and other campus administrators and faculty will have to make many tough decisions. Collection analysis and development and acquisition policies will have to take into account access alternatives, the appropriateness of shared resources on a regional, national or international basis, de-selection as well as selection, and choice of format.

More broadly, higher education and many of the scholarly disciplines need to review the scope, purpose and use of scholarly publication and the implications of the new information technologies. For example, should print journal publication by faculty (the publish-or-perish syndrome) still play its traditional role in faculty selection, retention, promotion and reward? Has technical publishing become too much a seller's market?

Higher education, the publisher, and the author/reader must confront the issues of intellectual property rights and the impact of copying, electronic replication, and the ease, value and convenience of individual reproduction of copyrighted materials for reference and teaching.

We must begin to contemplate how we can use technology to change our curricula and our educational structures and to serve the needs of future student bodies. We must decide whether our focus should be on applying technology to current organisation, facilities, faculty and traditional concepts of 'higher education', or on applying it to the needs that the social changes wrought by this IT itself will create. Just as the bricks and mortar of the library and its physical archive of containers of information will be transformed gradually to provide extramural services to scholars, similar transformations will take place in the institutions of higher learning as a whole.

Academic institutions must rethink their organisational approach to change. Planning for both the utilisation and the impact of changing information technologies must be done on an integrated basis that involves the academic administration, faculty, administrative services, libraries, computer centres and media centres. Traditional structures developed over generations have done much to provide autonomy and intellectual freedom. But these traditional structures were developed at a relatively slow pace over long periods of time. Today's environment is changing rapidly, and traditional structures may not be suited to planning and decision-making that assumes a high degree of support for what I would call an integrated information infrastructure, or what some, describing a more physical concept, refer to as the 'wired campus'. If we do not integrate, we will find ourselves with a confusion of differences and incompatibilities of software and hardware, redundancy of effort and investment, and the existence of multiple sources of information that are either unknown or are not readily accessed outside a narrow group.

And while I firmly believe creative imagination and energy thrive in the smallest possible unit in any organisation, there is a growing need for researchers and scholars to communicate with their peers and the world by radio, telephone, teleconferencing, electronic mail and electronic bulletin boards, and to transmit drafts, reviews and research results in electronic form long before they are formally published. This need will be particularly strong in those fields where change is very rapid, as it is in certain of the sciences and technological areas.

To summarise, it seems to me that those involved in designing and implementing higher education strategies to exploit the benefits and deal with the impact of IT trends must include the following on their agenda:

- Technology planning, assessment and transfer.

- Campus-wide integrated planning for the utilisation of all the information resources, both on the campus and offsite, that will be a part of the campus environment.

- Involve the faculty heavily in the process.

- Re-examining the role of the campus computer centre in the broader concept of information processing and its relationship with other information resources.

- Planning for the transformation of the library's role in the electronic information environment while recognising its unique role in preserving our cultural heritage.

- Exploring new avenues of inter-institutional collaboration and research, and academic networking on a national and international scale.

- Rethinking budgeting and financial analysis in the light of changing investment patterns brought about by rapidly changing technological trends in all areas affecting the university.

- Providing the faculty and support staff with appropriate training and technical support to ensure hands-on application of technologies in both the planning and operational stages, particularly as we apply the technologies to the teaching, learning and research functions.

- Pressing for the adoption and observance of standards in applying the new information technologies, not only at the campus level but also at the inter-institutional, national and international levels. (This will frequently require the academic community to put pressure on vendors themselves to adopt common standards that permit transfer of software.)

- Supporting fresh approaches to balancing intellectual property rights with the educational imperative of full and broad access to information.

- Re-examining the traditional approaches to print publication in recognising and rewarding scholarship, in the light of the potential impact of both current publication trends and the impact of new information technologies.

- Providing greater inter-institutional effort to support development of the new teaching and learning tools that will be possible from the application of the new information technologies.

What I am suggesting is that we rethink our 'time block' approach to education and that we make a concerted and integrated effort to plan for change in higher education, with care and concern for what happens to the student participants before they come to the university and after they leave it. This will not be easy. We know that organisations, like people, resist change. Inertia is a powerful force in academic environments. As Derek Bok, the President of Harvard University, has humorously reflected, it seems like many on the campus feel that nothing should ever be done for the first time. It is clear to me that while caution should be exercised and band-wagon urges should be controlled, we must act on what we know – or what we think we know. We can't simply wait for Godot. Or, to put it another way, if we do not inform ourselves and act boldly and decisively, our 'brushstrokes' will remain forever rooted in their pedestal; we will never have the joy of seeing them take flight.

References

[1] Fisher, F. D. Higher education circa 2005: more higher learning but less college. *Change,* January/February 1987, 40-5.

[2] Ibid., 40-1.

[3] Haeger, J. W. Unfinished business: computers, libraries and East Asian societies. A paper presented at the 4th US-Japan Conference on Libraries & Information Science in Higher Education. Racine, Wisconsin, 4 October 1988.

Research Activities and Information [summary of lecture]

Professor R M Hayes, *University of California, Los Angeles*

The professional context

My comments, while they will encompass broad issues of academic strategic planning and the needs of scholars, will be set in the context of professional imperatives, corollary commitments, and operational realities that determine the librarian's response to management of scholarly information. I will first describe that professional perspective, as I see it.

To do so, I will define the 'library' both narrowly – to represent the library as we now know it – and broadly – to cover the entire range of information resources under an all-encompassing 'library of the future'. The latter encompasses a wide range of administrative agencies responsible for information resources – the library (narrowly defined), the media centre, computer facilities, data archives, film archives, information centres. In fact, as I will explore, the magnitude of investment in information resources is surely two to three times that represented by the library, narrowly defined. Among the strategic planning issues, of course, are many concerned with the administrative arrangements among this array of agencies. Should there be an 'information czar'; should they all be blanketed into the library, making it de facto broadly defined as the campus information agency; should they function independently but with some level of coordination? In this talk I will not try to deal with these administrative issues, important as they are (though I am personally convinced that the distributed but coordinated approach is the best). What I do want to do is highlight the issues that make the distinction important.

The professional imperatives

The librarian has two professional imperatives:

- Preservation of the record

- Providing access to the record and its contents

Underlying these is the view that the record of the past is important, indeed that information contained in that record has value to the future sufficient to justify the costs in preservation and in providing access. One of the strategic planning problems of greatest moment is reconciling the dynamic tension between these two imperatives.

Given the professional imperatives, there are several evident commitments within the profession that serve as substantial determinants of its responses to policy issues and to the dynamic tension between them. I view them as natural consequences of the imperatives, since they are continuations of the underlying view that information is important. On the surface of it, these commitments all have specific relevance to the imperative of access to the record and thus figure in the broadened arena rather than the narrower one. I will comment on each of them:

- Open availability of information: needs and barriers

- Free service: capital investments and operating expense

- Cooperation: actual costs and perceived benefits

Clearly, even though I am focusing on the professional vision, we must recognise economic and physical realities since, of course, while there are the professional 'imperatives' and corollaries to them, that by no means makes them absolutes. Indeed, it is impossible to preserve every record, so selection is a critical professional responsibility. Any library must limit the range of users and uses to which it provides access; otherwise the responsibilities it has to its source of funding would be eroded. These together make cooperation a necessity, since otherwise the professional imperatives could not be met. And libraries leave to other agencies (such as the bibliographic utilities and the indexing and abstracting services) the creation of many of the tools for access. The reasons here are almost purely economic; it would be impossible for each library to incur the investments required by these tools of access.

The academic strategic planning context

I will then turn to the identified topic of my talk – Research Activities and Information. I will do so by discussing the general task of strategic planning for information resources in the research university, based largely on my experience in continuing effort at UCLA with that objective. There are some significant

43

issues that I hope to discuss that are revealing of the reality of planning and the priorities of faculty and administration.

The most important point, in that respect, is I think that most of what I have said about the librarian's imperatives, commitments, and operational realities apply not only to the library – whether narrowly or broadly defined – but with at least equal vigour to the university as a whole. The university's imperative is also based on the view that information is important to both the society and the individual. There is a professional commitment to 'information' as deep as that of the librarian. It is seen in the traditions of both education and research, with open access to published information a crucial component of both.

The process of strategic planning

I will review the goals and objectives of strategic planning, both in general and in terms of specific goals. I will discuss the relationships among levels of planning – strategic, tactical, and operational. I will discuss the management of project studies. The latter, especially, have been predicated on the view that the identification of faculty needs, as they see them, should be the foundation.

The studies sponsored within academic departments have included the following: School of Management, School of Law, Graduate School of Library and Information Science, School of Medicine (Departments of Neurology, Pediatrics, Radiology), Center for African Studies, Program in Applied Linguistics, Center for Latin American Studies, Center for Medieval and Renaissance Studies, School of Engineering (Department of Chemical Engineering), Institute for Social Science Research, Department of Psychology, College of Fine Arts (Music Department and Theater and Television), School of Architecture and Urban Planning. And others will be initiated during the coming year.

In general, these faculty-generated projects relate to the broad definition of the library, not the narrow one; they focus on the information and means for creation of it and access to it. None in fact has identified or even recognised the role of selection, acquisition, and preservation.

The result is that the strategic planning process must generalise from the specific of the individual projects. And there has been clear demonstration of generic problems, ones that should provide the basis for university-wide strategic planning. I will mention four that seem representative of categories of needs:

44

- Digitised images

- Electronic mail

- Database consultation

- Project management

Beyond these faculty-generated studies, several have been initiated related specifically to the information resources, facilities, and functions themselves. And, finally, there are studies concerned with the university administrative issues.

External issues: economic, political and social policies affecting the university

In the course of establishing the framework for strategic planning, several issues have been identified that relate primarily to factors outside the university itself and yet which have dramatic effect upon the ability of faculty and information professionals to use information resources effectively in carrying out the university's responsibilities. These external factors need to be identified and means created by which the university's needs and obligations can be recognised in the social, economic, and political processes that lead to policy decisions at a national and state level.

- Changing methods of publication and distribution

- Relationships with the information industry

- Restrictions on 'open access to information'

- Integrity of reference

45

The Changing Economics of Information: an Industry View

David Summers, *Butterworth (Telepublishing) Ltd*

Occasionally I am reminded with a jolt of the changes that have occurred in the publishing industry in the past twenty years. Then I would not have called it an industry, but thought of it rather as a trade; still small, intimate and, on this side of the Atlantic, at least, relatively immune from corporate ownership. Today publishing is one of the stock market's hottest areas, as undervalued assets take on new significance. Gentlemanly practices have been replaced by those of professional management.

Recently I revisited the printer where I went for induction training. The state of the art composition technology of 1966 is now consigned to the firm's museum, ironwork painted green and once-moving parts polished lovingly. On the shop floor where once there was the frenzied noise of monotype and linotype keyboarding machines, there is now silence as operators 'key in' manuscripts at computer terminals, listening to music through their headphones. The workforce is a fifth of the size it was then and twice as efficient.

In order to understand the direction in which publishing is moving, it is important to understand the changes of the past two decades because contained in those changes are the seeds for the trends of the next decade.

Review of current trends

English has become accepted as the international language. Twenty years ago, firms such as Longman and Heinemann were starting to tap the enormous but still latent market of English as a Foreign Language. That market is now booming with vigorous competition between British and American publishers, and governments too, as to whether the world shall learn English or American English. From the universities' point of view, those disciplines which demand an international language use English. English replaced German as the language of science after World War II. No longer do sixth formers learn scientific German. Libraries have been able to rationalise their journal holdings by standardising on English language publications and cease subscribing to an ever-increasing number of foreign language publications. The result has been that foreign authors have chosen to write in English for international publication and foresake their native languages. This, in turn, has led to the increasing number of foreign publishers who are choosing to publish in the English language because their own markets are too small or the disciplines in which they wish to publish are international.

The number of publications has increased as the public becomes increasingly literate and as books become more user-friendly by improved design and text editing. The growth in new titles and editions recorded in the United Kingdom is growing at present by 10 000 per decade and is estimated to be 60 000 a year by 1990. Universities will continue to participate in the formation of a rapidly expanding knowledge base as the number of academics internationally increases, as books cross frontiers with more ease and as academics of standing emerge in what have hitherto been academically low grade countries. Academic and technical works from India and Korea, for instance, have to be treated with a respect which was not accorded to them twenty years ago. We can expect to see wider circulating literature from Russia and China. It is no longer enough to scan English and American literature and universities have to face the challenge of interacting with more diverse knowledge bases.

The value added to information by publication has acquired an enhanced premium. Twenty years ago, published information was classified by format and valued on that basis. Thus, a major law text was compared critically in cost with a Penguin reprinted novel. In both books and journals, there have been major changes in the structure of pricing and perception of value largely because of the economic need to survive. The economic circumstances of the 1970s led to a revaluing of information: the contents of books were valued rather than their format. This enabled publishers to price their goods with a realism which had not existed since World War II and, in part, was aided by the decision to decimalise the currency at a time of rising inflation.

The last decade, in particular, has seen a continuous trend towards shorter print runs. This is principally a factor of the market. University textbooks are no longer, in the UK at least, printed in the substantial numbers they once were due to changing teaching methods and reduced export potential to the USA and the Commonwealth. Students are not now expected to buy two or three textbooks, partly for cost reasons, but also because the method of teaching has changed with less emphasis on the course book and more on a range of reading from materials. Monographs have declined sharply as lecturers stopped buying personal copies and relied instead on library copies as a response to rising prices. Libraries find themselves torn between buying books and journals, with journals now accounting for 70% of all library budgets. The growth of the journal as an information medium has been a particular feature of the last two decades, although there are some industry observers who would maintain that the journal sector has now moved from growth into maturity.

The number of publishers operating in particular subject areas has grown. This has given the market the benefit of choice, but has also reduced print runs and increased prices as more publishers go after a limited market. School publishing, medicine and law have been good examples. The range has, of course, given more opportunities to academics to get their works published and, in many cases, increased competition has created a substantially improved product with skilful use of colour, design, and text structure.

Competition from America was felt particularly in the 1960s. The American textbook received a welcome in many universities, and still does. However, America is perhaps no longer regarded as the sole source of texts principally because of the structure of teaching in American courses and the recognition that there are cultural as well as course differences. English academics have also found difficulty in adjusting to the concept of writing to a scheme dictated by the market which has been such a feature of the American 'managed' book.

The 1960s were the Robbins era. Universities, libraries and student numbers grew. Money was cheap, inflation low. It was a good time for higher education and academic publishing. In the past decade, we have seen a changing fashion in areas for study with 'employment subjects' attracting the largest numbers. We have also seen the impact of economies in teaching staff, library budgets and research facilities. Academics have been far more purposeful in their authorship, writing for their curriculum vitae rather than their students. The new emphasis on allocation of costs in departments has made it more difficult for academics to get appropriate secretarial resources for helping them with their publications.

University budgets are static or cut back and the publisher now looks to the world of industry, business and the professions for an increasing volume of his business. Publishers now spend increasing amounts of their marketing budgets on targetting these sectors, whereas once they might have been content to ignore them by concentrating on the growing academic market. The university market will receive proportionately less attention than it used to as budgets and student numbers reduce.

Knowledge has become more accessible. Foreign books cross frontiers more easily, though piracy in books has been very much a feature of our times to the detriment of everyone. Computerised bibliographic databases give better access to publications by subject. University bookselling has become more positive with the growth of the campus bookshops and better stock control methods.

The state of the publishing industry

Writing this paper ten years ago, a publisher would have presented a gloomy front. At that time, the depression in the economy was leading to a sharply accelerating decline in sales of books, cancellation of subscriptions to journals, redundant stocks, redundant staff, high print costs and the prospect of the book being replaced by 'something electronic'.

The industry has survived in good health because it has become leaner and fitter. It is more marketing orientated, discriminating more than ever in the material it publishes and tailoring that material to specific needs. It is also using a printing industry which has undergone a total transformation in its cost base and which, by its adoption of lower manning and new composition and printing and binding technology, has enabled British publishers to continue to publish vigorously and competitively. It is also continuing to market more internationally using a wider range of outlets and to be less insular. Restructuring of the industry has also brought it the benefit of financial resources and size to inject increasing amounts into research and international marketing.

Twenty years ago, the industry could be likened to a large number of small nation states, mostly privately owned. Now they are increasingly owned by conglomerates. Publishers are attractive because they use relatively little capital and plant, have good cash flow and a product which is infinitely adaptable. Access to information, the ability to manipulate it and then distribute it through a variety of controlled distribution channels is at least as important as owning the basic information itself in today's society. In recent years, the recognition among publishers that to survive they must become the dominant publishers in a niche market has brought about a rationalisation of activity. Not only have publishers restricted their activities to their main markets in order to rationalise costs of marketing, but the conglomerates who, in some cases, owned them have in turn rationalised their publishing holdings and determined which principal activity they should pursue. Conglomerates like Tilling and BTR shed

Heinemann to concentrate on manufacturing activities; Reed shed its other businesses to become a publisher. The field is exciting and at times resembles a game of 'Happy Families'. Will the world be dominated by ten publishing groups by 2000 who have control over multi-range communications? The publishing industry has become glamorous to the Stock Exchange over the past decade because of the value of information it handles. There will be a number of major moves during the next five years which will leave today's state of play unrecognisable.

The impact of new media

What then are the factors that should particularly concern the universities? Firstly, the conviction that many felt ten years ago that the book was about to be replaced by electronic media has been massively tempered. Whilst there has been growth in online systems and considerable interest in other new technologies such as CD-ROM, there is, as yet, no sign that the next five years will see a major shift away from print-on-paper technology. There can be few, if any, publishers operating in the university market for whom the turnover from their electronic publishing exceeds 1% of their total turnover. Experiments in producing online journals have foundered and students have been barred from searching widely online because of the telecommunications costs involved. The management of online costs in research will continue to be a growing factor in university budgeting.

Technology will continue to loosen some of the controls which have checked the flow of information. The titles listed in Whitaker for 1986 emanated from 10 800 publishers. Of these, no more than 1900 could be called major houses. The remainder were small institutional or even mono-publication houses each applying their own criteria to justifying publication. On-demand techniques involving laser printing are creating many more opportunities for self-publishing, with the possibility of everyman becoming his own printer and publisher. This trend needs careful monitoring since it offers opportunities for by-passing the publisher's vital role as gatekeeper. In America, on-demand publishing is breathing new vitality into many university press activities.

Factors in the university market

The buying power of the library is crucial to publishers embarking on a post-graduate publication programme. Libraries abandoned the policy of stocking student textbooks in quantity a decade ago. That was a welcome and necessary move. More recently though the development of interlibrary loans has challenged the commercial assumptions of publishers. Whatever efficiencies there may be in one library buying and others borrowing from it, the fact is that the market will drop as market distribution is taken over by librarians and the consequences will be just as serious as those arising from copying techniques.

Two issues which have a bearing on information economics are again being rehearsed: the introduction of VAT and the abolition of the Net Book Agreement. The principal impact of both of these is on the student sector. The former, successfully resisted by the publishing industry in 1986, now appears to be very much in the hands of Brussels in the run up to 1992, whereas the second would appear to rest upon the acumen of a bookseller to challenge this Agreement which has imposed Resale Price Maintenance on books with the authority of the Courts since 1956. At first sight its abolition could lead to lower prices for student textbooks and competition between campus booksellers. University administrators may well have to reconsider the terms of their contract with their campus bookseller if they can no longer offer any form of guarantee about exclusive trading on campus.

It could also be accompanied by renewed determination by publishers to sell direct to their end markets as booksellers continue to concentrate on stocking faster moving, recently published titles rather than keeping a range of backlist titles.

Conclusions

There is, then, no doubt that over the next decade we shall continue to see rapid growth in the base of information with which universities and societies deal and that that base will become ever more international. If anything, markets are likely to become more fragmented unless there is greater standardisation of courses in the universities and print numbers will continue to decline. This is a direct response to a market in which copyright is circumvented and sales lost by photocopying, networking and downloading. Advanced printing techniques do, however, make it feasible for publishers with lower overheads to continue to publish texts for minority interests.

Journal subscriptions can be expected to decline further as assessment of the value of publications is made more rigorous and this will introduce conservatism into the launch of new journals as publishers have to be prepared to make more uncertain investment for much longer periods.

The trends of the next decade are in place; more information, high prices, smaller print numbers, more critical perception of value, more competition for authors and the student market with increasing interest in the UK from European publishers as well as American. The book and the journal are unlikely to be displaced by new technologies, although we can expect a gradual move towards data capture on compact disk.

The Changing Economics of Information: a Library/Information Service View

Professor Neil McLean, *Polytechnic of Central London*

One of the greatest difficulties in addressing the problems associated with the economics of information, irrespective of the viewpoint, is the lack of any consensus on how to measure information. Definitions of information invariably end up being too broad or too narrow for the purposes of practical application. I have been influenced considerably in my own thinking over the past year by a book written by Robert S. Taylor, entitled *Value-Added Processes in Information Systems* [1]. He begins with the assumption that 'information transfer is an intensely human process' and adopts, therefore, what he terms a 'user-driven approach' to the organisation of information systems. In doing so he asks three fundamental questions [2]:

1. What does an information system do for human beings to justify its costs?

2. Can we relate the systems costs (value added in the economist's terms) to the user enhancements added by the system (value added in the context of [this] book)?

3. What will be the cost in time and effort and money that users sitting in particular environments with particular problems must invest to obtain user information from any particular system?

I have begun on this somewhat theoretical note because the changes being brought about by the application of IT to information provision and use require a rethink of the basic perspectives which have informed management decisions over the past few decades.

Libraries have been regarded as the cornerstone of information provision in higher education for many years. Most successful institutions built up substantial collections and the dependence of the academic community on this library resource meant that it was a key political and financial element in the institutional strategy.

Success was measured primarily in terms of the size of the collection, whether it be monographs or periodicals. The fixed costs in terms of overheads and the implicit ongoing costs of retaining periodical subscriptions meant that libraries were able to expand their proportion of the institutional resource base through the 1960s and into the 1970s. This was a content-driven model which was dominated by input costs. There was little or no attention paid to outputs of the library system. The high point of this long-established policy was reached somewhere in the early 1970s.

The rapid development of computerisation, later to be subsumed by IT , engulfed libraries at a relatively early stage. This was no accident; the first phase of computerisation was good at handling transactional business and libraries adapted computers to the high volume traffic generated by their cataloguing and circulation processes. There was an evolutionary development including in-house batch systems, in-house online systems, cooperative systems and finally stand-alone turnkey systems. The arrival of the stand-alone turnkey systems epitomised the peak of what I call 'the control phase' of the information revolution. The technology was sufficiently sophisticated to permit the development of highly efficient control systems which gave library managers a degree of autonomy within the institution. In one important respect there has been a move beyond the control phase. Access to the library catalogue, using a public enquiry module and the institutional communications network is now commonplace. But this trend is still essentially a by-product of the control system and it does not represent a basic change in the means of information provision and access.

The recent studies on the state of the art of library automation in member states of the European Community indicate that UK institutions of higher education have outstripped all their European counterparts and indeed all other types of libraries in the application of library automation. Given the constant complaints about under-funding, this may come as a surprise to some, but it is an indisputable fact. This achievement has produced a major new line of expenditure in the financial process. The recurrent costs of maintaining these control systems is now a permanent feature of financial planning and it has been accompanied by a continuous battle to find a more stable process for the capital replacement of the systems as they become obsolete. Whilst there has been some success in formulating such a policy within the university sector, the public sector has, as yet, no policy whatsoever.

In parallel with these developments there has been a growing use of external electronic information services. These services have now been offered in major academic libraries for well over a decade. But the growth over the past five years in the use of these services has been relatively slow and the total expenditure on the purchase of electronic information services remains a very small proportion of the total library revenue budget. For example, in polytechnics during 1986-87, the proportion of the materials budget spent on online searches was only 2.74%. Why is this so? It could be that they are, and will continue to be, peripheral to user requirements and the market has reached saturation point. It could be that they are still too complex to use and the necessity of a skilled intermediary limits use. It could be that the information content is not sufficiently geared to use within higher education. It could be that libraries simply do not encourage use. It could be that the price is still too expensive when compared with manual sources. Or it could be that there are no proper charging/pricing mechanisms in place within the institution.

I suspect there is some truth in all these speculations and a root cause of the difficulties is the library view of the development and operation of electronic information services. The tendency is to see the expansion of electronic information services as an extension of the control phase where management and control is firmly entrenched with library managers. This is allied to the concept that users should not, in the main, be expected to pay except in the case of researchers with external funding. But it appears to be a policy doomed to failure and a complete review is required. So from the rather narrow perspective of the library manager, the threat of financial dislocation within the library domain has loomed large for the past few years. The rapid increase in book and periodical prices, the fall in institutional revenue bases, an increasing commitment to recurrent costs of automated systems, larger numbers of users, the high price of electronic information services, the steady increase in staff costs, all figure prominently in annual reports. These threats are undoubtedly real but statistics on library expenditure suggest that the problems are not quite what they seem. I shall use national UK polytechnic library statistics to demonstrate my points because they represent the sector with which I am most familiar [3].

The figures in Tables 1 and 2 show that over the last five years the quantitative inputs to library systems and the proportional expenditure on the major inputs have remained remarkably stable, given the apparent financial instability within the polytechnic sector and the changes taking place as a result of the use of IT. The figures certainly do not indicate any substantial reallocation of resources within existing budgets. The percentage spent on automation has risen steadily and it appears to be at the expense of materials rather than staff. This figure tends to be somewhat unreliable because the costs included in the automation expenditure vary considerably according to institutional arrangements. For instance, some institutions apportion overheads such as maintenance, telecommunications and networking to cost centres such as libraries, and others do not. The lack of standard practices in this area lead to gross distortion in comparative statistics.

All figures in the tables are expressed as the mean value of reported responses including zero. The total number of institutions is thirty.

Table 1   Quantitative inputs

	Periodical Titles	Books	Interlibrary Loans	Online Searches	Staff
1986/87	2245	12334	6042	331	55.12
1985/86	2201	13153	5637	287	53.58
1984/85	2248	12858	5621	255	53.77
1983/84	2349	13775	5923	213	54.43
1982/83	2269	16626	5567	232	52.66

Table 2   Expenditure
(expressed as a percentage of total
library expenditure)

	Materials	Automation	Salaries
1986/87	33	5.71	54.91
1985/86	35.85	5.29	53.38
1984/85	33.96	4.82	55.87
1983/84	34.43	4.06	56.11
1982/83	35.63	4.07	52.50

When viewed from yet another perspective, the size of library expenditure as a proportion of the institutional gross expenditure, the situation does not seem to be all that bad.

Table 3   Expenditure
(expressed as a percentage of gross
institutional expenditure)

1986/87	4.85
1985/86	4.50
1984/85	4.80
1983/84	4.59
1982/83	4.61

But the key to the immediate problems lies not with the actual inputs but with the numbers of customers. Table 4, which expresses figures in terms of expenditure per full-time equivalent student (FTE), shows a very different trend. It is not necessary to apply cost inflation to this table to see that expenditure per FTE is rapidly losing ground.

Table 4   Expenditure per FTE (in £'s)

	Total Expenditure	Total Materials	Books
1986/87	147.88	49.71	23.27
1985/86	138.82	48.24	22.99
1984/85	138.43	47.51	21.80
1983/84	153.10	45.97	23.01
1982/83	153.10	53.22	29.84

So what conclusions can be drawn from these illustrative statistics? It appears that polytechnic libraries are locked into fairly traditional budget heads with staff and periodicals being dominant and apparently inflexible. The proportion of the institutional expenditure remains stable but the amount spent per head of the population is falling in real terms.

It seems necessary to place this analysis of library expenditure in a wider context if we are to formulate more positive strategies for the development of information services. The rapid expansion of the application of IT in research and teaching has been dominated by two main forces: the computer centre or computing services, and initiatives by individuals or groups of academic staff. The economic, political and technological elements that drive this development make it a fierce battleground. Throughout the 1970s the computer centres were dominant in both the planning and the provision of IT services because of the dependency on mainframe machines. The major arguments concerning capital investment centred on the upgrades of these central processors. But the rapid emergence of distributed processing power, together with the possibilities of sophisticated communications networks changed the balance of power and planning became much more a bartering process. Individual members of staff at both the research and teaching level were able to acquire sufficient processing power and expertise to develop facilities independently of the central resources and this has led to strong pleas for a devolution of finance, decision making and forward planning, based on the technological rationale of distributed processing power. Because of this multifaceted approach to IT development, resources have been acquired and deployed in an unplanned and uncoordinated fashion in most institutions. Whilst some statistics are available on the expenditure of central computer services the real expenditure on IT is impossible to quantify at the present time. Within the UK, institutions are at various stages of evolution in this particular process. Some have retained the older style central budgeting and planning process, some have established a devolved system of cost centres and many have a mixture of the two. But whatever the style of management the proportion of institutional expenditure on IT is growing rapidly.

How then can libraries position themselves in this wider struggle? It is now generally accepted that libraries can no longer formulate resource strategies in isolation from developments within the institution, particularly in the field of IT . The complexity of such developments probably means that no single model can serve as a guide to future practice. It is, however, important that we attempt to map the critical factors.

At the most general level we need to take account of user requirements, the functions necessary to support these requirements and the resources needed to carry out these functions. In developing this operational model it is essential that we map the interaction of three strategic elements, computing, communications and information content, on the operational model. The interaction of these three strategic elements is the key to planning for the 1990s. In general the aim will be to provide the widest possible access to resources through computer and communications networks both nationally and internationally, to provide a distributed computing environment that links workstations, personal computers and larger machines in all buildings regardless of operating system through open system interconnection architecture; and to provide a range of information databases including textual and numeric data, documents, images, video and audio information. The library will have a key role in developing such a strategy, if it can relate to the development of institutional policies for the application of IT to teaching and research. What then should be the nature of library input to this debate? It is highly desirable that a model is developed which moves on from the collection-based content model to one that concentrates on the user requirements for access to information. This is not to say that libraries should abandon existing practices or that they should throw away the print collections but rather that they should explore planning mechanisms from a different perspective so as to permit a more positive input into institutional debates on resource strategies.

In order to achieve this goal it is necessary to develop a model that embraces the user and the use environment, the systems through which information is to be delivered, the information content of these systems and the means by which the users can best utilise the output of both the systems and the information content. It is at this point that I return to the ideas of Robert S. Taylor. He has developed what he calls the User-Driven Model which is depicted in Figure 1 [4].

It is important that we explore the use of such a model, because the way in which users access and use information is undergoing a complete transformation. The growth of distributed computing and institutional communication networks has shifted the focus to the development of workstation facilities and personal information systems. From the workstation any user can reasonably expect to interrogate the library catalogue through the public enquiry module, reserve an item, order an interlibrary loan, interrogate other library catalogues, interrogate commercial databases, interrogate textual and numeric databases held within the institutions, call up image, video and audio information held internally or externally, merge files and apply the information as part of other applications software. Within such a concept the library moves from being a passive supplier to that of an active facilitator serving the needs of the end user. The implementation of such a concept has profound implications for the economics relating to the supply and demand of information within the institution.

Figure 1   The User-Driven Model

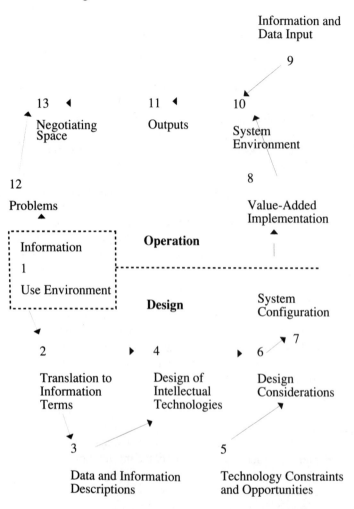

Information and
Data Input

9

13 ◄   11 ◄   10

Negotiating   Outputs   System
Space   Environment

12   8

Problems   Value-Added
                                 Implementation

Information   **Operation**

1

Use Environment

                                 System
                    Design   Configuration

                                        ▼ 7
2   ► 4   ► 6

Translation to   Design of   Design
Information   Intellectual   Considerations
Terms   Technologies

             3   5

Data and Information   Technology Constraints
Descriptions   and Opportunities

Because there are no rules in place to govern resource management in such an information-use environment, new models are necessary and they must be developed rapidly into working models if there is to be sensible institutional planning.

The attraction of the Taylor-type model is that it imposes potential discipline on this planning process and it seeks a way beyond the content-driven and technology-driven models. It acknowledges the importance of the use environment and the emergence of the end user as the key element in the development of IT. There is, however, a great deal of work to be done in developing practical techniques for the measurement of value-added implementations.

From the library viewpoint it is crucial that there be a thorough review of systems configuration to see how the large investment in stand-alone systems can be enhanced to extend user access to information other than that relating to the stock held within the institution. The development of online public access catalogues networked throughout institutions has been practically and symbolically an important first step in the extension of user access. But there is a variety of technologies available to achieve such a goal and the interfaces between the technologies and the cost benefits of each option require continuous experimentation and review.

As part of this evaluation the concept of value-added implementation is an important, if difficult, one. Given that the user will, in effect, be developing personal information systems which have many of the same characteristics of the larger systems, the user criteria of choice as identified by Taylor become more specific: ease of use, noise reduction, quality, adaptability, time saving and cost saving. To meet these criteria potential improvements can be made in both system processes and in interfacing solutions, as shown in Figure 2 [5].

To achieve any or all of the tasks set out in the above diagram will require close collaboration between the technical experts and the information experts within the institution, and traditional organisational structures will have to be rethought to ensure optimal inputs to this task. But the crux of the whole process for libraries will be the reassessment of content policy to ensure the appropriate balance between in-house hardcopy monographs and periodicals, interlibrary loans, internal electronic information services and reliance on access to external electronic information services. There will be no hard-and-fast policies for

Figure 2

USER CRITERIA OF CHOICE	INTERFACE (Values Added)	SYSTEM (Value-Added Processes: Examples)
Ease of Use	Browsing Formatting Interfacing I (Mediation) Interfacing II (Orientation) Ordering Physical accessibility	Alphabetising Highlighting important terms
Noise Reduction	Access I (Item identification) Access II (Subject description) Access III (Subject summary) Linkage Precision Selectivity	Indexing Vocabulary control Filtering
Quality	Accuracy Comprehensiveness Currency Reliability Validity	Quality control Editing Updating Analysing and comparing data
Adaptability	Closeness to problem Flexibility Simplicity Stimulatory	Provision of data manipulation capabilities Ranking output for relevance
Time Saving	Response speed	Reduction of pro-cessing time
Cost Saving	Cost saving	Lower connect-time price

information content provision over the next decade because of the volatile nature of communications and computing technologies, hence the importance of a model which can embrace a range of variables.

The model as depicted concentrates on changes in particular user environments, but it is important to realise that there are comparable changes occurring in the traditional textual distribution chain involving authors, publishers, booksellers, wholesale distributors, libraries, documentation centres and database producers, because the computing and communication technologies produce increasing options for the creation, production and distribution of information. It is not the mission of this paper to deal with this particular process, but it is important that institutional managers realise the interdependence between the two processes and realise also that market forces in the publishing sector often dictate the pace of institutional development. Volume sales are critical to the commercial sector and these can only be developed and sustained if there is a greater number of users, not only with access to potential new products and services, but with an ability to pay for them.

But regardless of the balance between the traditional hardcopy resource, the in-house electronic services and the reliance on external electronic services, the output is a range of information products, systems and services which have to be regarded as resources which can be controlled and managed productively and, as Taylor says, this demands answers to the following questions :

- Who acquires, organises and transmits what information?

- By what means?

- At what cost?

- To whom?

- To what effect?

There is now a substantial body of literature on information resource management although it is, as yet, stronger in theory than in practice. But a start can be made on the management of visible assets with a gradual move towards models which assess and measure information 'outcomes' rather than information 'outputs' in the more mechanistic sense.

From the library point of view it is inevitable that there will be a major shift in information resource use and management within the institution and this demands a shift in resource allocation. The political struggle which this process engenders is intense, and in some cases decisions are being made on the basis of political 'muscle' rather than rational resource management.

The existing allocation to traditional library resources has, as illustrated earlier, remained relatively stable over the past five years in at least one sector of higher education and that is likely to remain so, provided the present levels of productivity can be sustained. But the electronic campus can only evolve if there is a redeployment of resources within faculties or if the students contribute more towards the cost of information services. The extent of end user access and the means by which that is controlled and financed are key issues for the 1990s. If the library is to be at the forefront of this debate it must be seen as an agent of change and a facilitator of new services and products rather than a wounded giant seeking constant transfusions of resources to sustain a genteel poverty. The days of the stand-alone library are numbered but the day of the stand-alone end user is yet to come. It will take the energies of the institution as a whole, and not just the library, to map out the intervening years.

References

[1] Taylor, R. S. *Value-Added Processes in Information Systems.* Norward, N. J.: Ablex Publishing Corp., 1986.

[2] Ibid., 1.

[3] *Statistics of Polytechnic Libraries.* Council of Polytechnic Librarians. (Annual statistics covering the years 1982/83 to 1986/87.)

[4] Taylor, R. S., op.cit., 25.

[5] Ibid., 50.

The Electronic Campus – an Information Strategy: Organisation Issues

Ivan Sidgreaves, *Plymouth Polytechnic*

'.....it is the framework itself that changes with new technology, and not just the picture within the frame.'

Marshall McLuhan [1]

The concept of the 'electronic campus' and the potential it has not only to change fundamentally the process of education, but also to deinstitutionalise it, is one which requires a significant shift in our thinking if we are firstly to understand the opportunities it offers, and then as managers to use them in the best interests of our students and staff. The problem is not simply one of understanding and identifying the salient changes in the relevant technologies, nor recognising the convergence of service interests, but one which has the potential to impinge on every part of an institution's activities, its structure, its management, and, most importantly, its teaching and research. In the early 1970s, I attended a seminar which was concerned with identifying what some then saw as the necessary lines of demarcation to be drawn between librarians and educational technologists with regard to the creation, storage, and utilisation of audio-visual materials. Little of significance remains in my memory from that particular event, except for the fact that it was held on the shores of Lake Windermere, and that for me at least it demonstrated the utter futility of individuals working at the heart of the educational process who were actually set in opposition to each other for purely selfish and short-sighted reasons. I relate this incident, partly because I am quite certain that this is not a conference about who does what, but more because it seems only fair at the outset of this paper to lay down my credentials as someone committed to, and who has become increasingly involved in, the operation of inter-related services – library, computing, and educational technology – working in support of learning, teaching and research. However, as other colleagues have been asked to prepare case studies of individual institutions, my task is not to talk about my own institutional view of these issues, but to address some of the wider organisational implications of the electronic campus.

I do not propose to become involved in a discussion at first hand of the literature either of complex organisations or of organisational behaviour, though much of this seeks to evaluate and explain the impact of technology on organisational structures and on individual behaviour. In preparing this paper, however, I have found it helpful to refer to an article by Shaughnessy [2], in which he surveys that literature to explain and examine the impact of technology on the structure of libraries. He provides an excellent summary of some of the central issues, many of which I will be returning to in the course of this paper:

> That the structure of an organisation moulds itself to the demand of technology, few scholars doubt. Describing the precise nature of technology and documenting the effect of technology on structure, however, has been extremely difficult. One of the reasons for the difficulty is the fact that complex organisations are multivariate in nature. Their structures and operations are contingent upon a variety of factors, some of the more salient of which are size, the nature of the environments in which they operate, the values, needs and expectations of their members, and technology. But technology has increasingly been found to be the key variable in organisational analysis, affecting dimensions such as management style, design of individual jobs, worker specialisation and division of labour, levels of management, span of control and program specification, among others. In fact, technology has been found to affect the behaviour of all members of an organisation through its influence on work systems and its collective effect on social structures and group norms. Several research studies have also established that organisations employing sophisticated or advanced technologies are more affected than those with relatively stable and unchanging technologies.

> To the extent that an organisation's technology is well understood, predictable, routine and repetitive, a bureaucratic structure may be most effective. But where technology is non-routine, unstable, unpredictable, and non-repetitive, a bureaucratic or hierarchical structure may be dysfunctional. In the latter situation, more discretion is usually neeeded by lower level personnel, more interactions among various levels and coordinative mechanisms are required, and considerably higher levels of organisational responsiveness and flexibility are called for.

It would be useful to examine this thesis in rather greater detail as it might be applied to institutions of higher education. If, for example, we consider closely what has been happening in libraries and computing centres, we might conclude that the impact of technological change has had more effect on internal processes and procedures than on internal organisational structures, and certainly only rarely has it had any marked effect on institutions at large. This is the 'predictable, routine and repetitive' element of the Shaughnessy model. There is a commonly held view that in many libraries it is the technology which has had to adapt to the traditional structural divisions of operations between technical services and reader services. Shaughnessy's somewhat damning thesis is 'that library structures have not sufficiently changed to accommodate new technologies, and that this has resulted in poor utilisation of staff and user frustration.'

My brief, in the context of the electronic campus, is 'to cover concerns of organisational structures including the relationships between information activities and other administrative/support activities, institutional information management policies, and management of the distributed processing environment.' Whilst in considering the impact of the developing network technologies on the structure of institutions, it is not wholly necessary to explain in any detail the internal structure of support services, it would be useful as background to examine briefly the present pattern of organisational structures in higher education, and in particular the place of libraries, computing services and other support services, before moving to the concept of the electronic campus and the implications that that has for organisational change.

It would not be possible nor, indeed, particularly helpful to examine in detail the variety of models of institutional organisation existing in our universities and polytechnics. Such structures are often the result of an involved evolution, which has depended, inter alia, on local history, environmental factors, personalities, available resources, and external forces. Indeed, given the complexity of these variables, there are surprising similarities of structure between different institutions. Units of organisation such as faculties, schools, colleges, departments are familiar to us on both sides of the binary divide, whilst teaching groups, subject domains, and similar nomenclature, though to some little more than semantic variations on those traditional structures, are also recognisable. In the case of libraries and computing services in universities and polytechnics, though there may rarely be any significant difference in their place in the overall

67

institutional structure, increasingly there are variations in their perceived role and purpose. In organisational terms, they are generally established as free-standing units/departments, which in the case of all libraries and the majority of computing services are the responsibility of a chief librarian or computer services manager, who variously equates with a dean of faculty or head of department, and may even, in many universities, carry professorial status. They report to a library committee, computer user group, or some such similar body, and the librarian and computing manager will normally be ex officio members of Senate or Academic Board.

In the university sector, the range and type of libraries is considerable, ranging from those in Oxford and Cambridge, with their role as national collections, through the later civic foundations with significant collections, such as Birmingham, Leeds, Manchester, to those of more recent origin, including the 'technological' universities. With notable exceptions, their central purpose has been collection development in support of research and teaching. In pursuit of this objective, it was not unknown in the past for such libraries to attempt to purchase a single copy of everything published. The publishing explosion, reductions in funding, and scarcity of space has forced a reassessment of this particular approach, though for many collection development remains central and their custodial role dominates. The designation of polytechnics began in the early 1970s, and many have grown rapidly through mergers and amalgamations. Some libraries like Manchester and Newcastle have developed significant collections, and most have seen the relevance of developing multi-media collections. In general, however, there has been a recognition that apart from the impracticality of building large collections, information self-sufficiency no longer means that a library must own everything of potential use. Many polytechnic libraries and some of the universities have come to realise that it is more important to be able to access information when needed, and have harnessed a variety of new technologies to achieve their ends. At the same time, they have also laid greater emphasis on training their students in information handling skills.

There have been other developments of significance in polytechnic libraries. In the mid 1970s, Brighton and Plymouth created Learning Resource Centres, bringing together not only their library services, but also media production and educational development activities in a common organisational structure. The emphasis was firmly on the process of learning, with a strong focus on support both for the student as well as for the lecturer. The library collections were multi-media in nature, and reading rooms were designed to cope with a variety of patterns of learning and study, including those which made use of audio-visual equipment. More recently, the introduction of microcomputers has sought to give added emphasis to the library as a learning centre, but has also caused some to question the precise nature of the library's role in the field of IT. Other polytechnics have followed suit and have variously grouped learning support services together in this way, usually under the overall responsibility of the polytechnic librarian. It has to be said, however, that this is done more often as a consequence of resource constraint rather than because of educational expediency.

The development of institutional computing services has a more recent history in both sectors. Initially most machines were for research and were concentrated in a small number of institutions, but with the development of the technology they quickly found their way into most of the universities. In both universities and polytechnics, they were often at first closely associated with teaching departments, particularly mathematics and computing science, a fact which McLean [3] has suggested 'produced a high level of response in these particular areas...however, it may be inhibiting developments elsewhere in teaching departments simply because the dominance of pure computer expertise is often too narrow to perceive the more modest requirements of other teaching areas.' Despite this, other disciplines increasingly began to make demands on them. The early computing technology was bulky, highly complex and facilities usually had to be housed in a centre to which staff and students brought data to be processed, a task which initially was undertaken on their behalf. Computing staff were able to play out the role of the high priest interceding with the computing deity on behalf of the lesser mortals – staff and students. For the purpose of this paper it is not relevant to trace in any detail the technological developments of the intervening period, save to note the advent of the microcomputer, the developing communication technologies, the growth in multi-user online capability to mainframes and the availability of increasingly powerful software. Mainframe systems have benefitted from the miniaturisation of components, but have themselves become very powerful computing engines capable of performing increasingly complex functions.

As for the computing services themselves, they have had to change. Though most universities and polytechnics still run large central systems, there has also been a growth in distributed systems for teaching and research. In some cases these are linked into the central facility through a communications network, whilst in others they may be free-standing super minis or suites of microcomputers. Increasingly staff at the centre have had to cope with a bewildering variety of hardware and software, even in those institutions where policies on standardisation have attempted to control such developments. The technology has become more accessible to the non-expert, whose needs are often modest and can be met through word processing, spreadsheet and database management software, though with this has come the expectation of increased accessibility to facilities and a demand for staff development, and training in basic computer literacy. The role of computing staff is changing from that of intermediary to that of consultant and adviser on a wide range of systems and software.

Though in briefly examining support services, I have concentrated on libraries and computing centres, in some institutions there has also been a third support unit which has been more concerned with the development of new methods of teaching and learning. There are probably as many titles for such units as there are institutions, but the use of the term educational technology unit will probably be understood by most people. Their functions also vary considerably, but in general they have been concerned with the development of pedagogic skills, the production of audio-visual materials, both as an aid to the teacher and as a medium for learning, and the development of new educational delivery systems, particularly in the context of the needs of open and distance learning. Reference has already been made to Brighton and Plymouth polytechnics, where such units were an integral part of the Learning Resources Centre, but in other institutions they were often independent units with cross-institutional responsibilities. In the past few years, largely as a result of resourcing constraints, many such units have disappeared, perhaps somewhat curiously at a time when there is a renewed interest in the effectiveness of teaching skills, a growing interest in developing new approaches to teaching and learning, as a result of the growing demand for wider access to higher education, as well as the demand for continuing education through open and distance learning.

Though it has not been necessary thus far to concentrate in any detail on the developing information technologies, it might be helpful at this point to remind ourselves briefly of the elements which constitute the electronic campus, and the significance of the technological changes which make it a possibility. We are concerned with an electronic revolution which is fundamentally changing the ways information can be generated, stored and transferred. At its heart is the network, the telecommunication system which makes it possible for users to locate information or make use of specific services at remote locations. It may use a variety of technologies, including laser, microwave, and satellite to create local area networks (LANs), and provide access to wide area networks (WANs), and has the capacity to carry text, data, voice, and even video. For the user, whether they be academic, student, or administrator, access to the network will usually be via a personal computer (PC), either in the office, study place, or even via a modem from home. For the lecturer, access will be possible in the lecture theatre permitting him to display data, text or video as a teaching aid. The structure of the network will enable the user to call up information from both internal and external sources, to exchange information with colleagues in his own institution, or any others at a distance, including overseas, and to create his own personal databases as required.

With few notable exceptions, the central support services – library, computing and educational technology – have hitherto been developed in isolation from each other, and only rarely is there evidence of any inter-service cooperation. Computer-based library housekeeping systems were in the first instance introduced and managed without reference to the computing centre; libraries of audio-visual materials were developed independently of the main library collection; whilst in some institutions departmental libraries or departmental computing systems were developed in isolation from other institutional services, regardless of problems of duplication or incompatibility. Reflecting the Shaughnessy concept of the unstable environment, the roles and responsibilities of services, however, are becoming less clearly defined as the technologies develop, and break down some of the more easily recognised lines of responsibility between libraries and computing services, or central services as against those located in teaching departments. Libraries are becoming increasingly dependent on access to remote information sources via internal and external networks, whilst IT now pervades all aspects of learning, teaching and research. In the majority of institutions of higher education, however, the divisions between libraries, computing centres and educational technology units remain rigidly defined, emanating as they do from hierarchical structures of management, and any idea of planning their development in a more coordinated way is yet to be realised. We are moving into an era, however, when it will no longer be possible to consider these services in isolation from each other, or from the institution at

71

large, and where greater responsiveness and flexibility will be required. Structures which were put in place in the main as a response to the requirement of providing services at a single location are no longer appropriate. The concept of an electronic or wired campus will cause us to re-examine both the function and structure of these services, and their relationship to other institutional services, but even that will not be sufficient. With the development of new communication and information technologies it will be necessary to examine the total information strategy of an institution, and the implications that has, not just for central support services but also for all aspects of the institution's activities.

For the library, its role becomes less custodial, less that of simply mediating between the user and the printed word, and more that of accessing information from whatever sources may be appropriate, both within the confines of an institution and from the information world at large. It offers the possibilities of new storage techniques, and information processing systems such as CD-ROM, as well as the potential to communicate directly with user PCs through the network. The notion of a computing centre is rapidly disappearing, and in many institutions the concept of a computing service with responsibilities stretching beyond the confines of the central facilities has been developed. The challenges lie in the management of distributed systems, in the complexities of network technology, and in the increasing need to work more closely with teaching and research departments, institutional administration, as well as other support services. In the process of doing this the boundaries between libraries and computing centres are becoming increasingly blurred, as are those between central services and departmentally located services. Even the physical boundaries of library buildings and computing centres no longer represent the defined limits of these services, or the extent of their information responsibilities.

The whole focus of this paper thus far has been on support for the academic processes, but, in parallel, administrative services have also been developing IT-based systems in support of their work, many of which will necessarily impinge on the total information infrastructure of the institution. Registry functions, such as student academic records, transcripts, and exam results, may be handled electronically, centrally or at the level of faculty or department. Financial management systems are a concern not just at the centre, but increasingly for faculty and service managers. The divisions between academic and administrative are less clearly defined than they were, and their common interest in the development of institutional information systems means that developments cannot be tackled in total isolation from each other. However, before returning to that, it is necessary to consider in a little more detail some of the issues of management and of structure, both in terms of the institution and at the level of the central support services.

We are rapidly nearing a point, however, when the issue cannot simply be contained in a redefinition of the roles of library and computing services, necessary though that might well be, nor in a restructuring of their management within the institution. The opportunities of the electronic campus will have an impact on all aspects of an institution's work, and requires the development of an overall institutional information strategy. To return to Shaughnessy, we should remind ourselves 'that the more sophisticated the technology, the higher is the policy-making level involved.' At the same time, we might note that he also suggests that 'the more advanced and sophisticated the technology variable, the greater the need for flexible, responsive structures.'

Before returning, therefore, to details of organisational structure, it is important to stress the need for an institutional information strategy, which provides a defined framework within which developments can be coordinated and developed. It is no longer sufficient to regard information and IT simply as the province of specialists in libraries and computing services, because increasingly it will intrude into all aspects of an institution's life. The natural conclusion in some institutions will be that the issues implicit in the concept of the electronic campus are so fundamental that it will be necessary to identify someone at the most senior level to take an overview of all such developments. In others, the issues will be regarded as so complex, broad and all-pervading that they must in consequence be at the heart of the decision-making processes of the institution, whilst elsewhere they will be left to another suitably identified forum. Decisions about the nature of organisational structures depend on a number of variables, and it is likely that different institutions will choose to solve the problem in a variety of ways, but at the heart of this is the requirement that the information strategy be given an institutional focus.

Whatever else, it is probable in most institutions that the convergence of interests which are a direct result of developments in IT will require a reappraisal of the relationship between computing, library, and educational technology units. The concern is not simply one of defining roles, or of the way they interact, but also of their continuing central role versus the opportunities offered by

73

the technologies for dispersing those roles to faculties and departments. It is clearly not in any institution's interests, and specifically against the interests of students and staff, for these central services to work in opposition to each other, or to develop in total isolation either from each other or from the institution as a whole. It is increasingly difficult to separate the information role and the technological role, nor may it be in anybody's interest to do so, a situation which Lynne Brindley [4] suggests might be best served by a 'high tech to no tech integration of our support services....focused around the concept of a looser network of support, involving skills and teamwork across boundaries from both traditional library/information services and computing services.'

Some institutions, on both sides of the binary line, have already put structures in place which aim to avoid problems of duplication and isolation in the development of these support services. Whilst we might usefully examine a number of organisational models which are aimed principally at the better coordination of such services, individual institutions will inevitably make decisions on matters of management and structure according to a variety of factors. There is clearly no best design, no ideal. Each is dependent on local environmental factors, personalities, the institution's historical development, its overall aims and objectives, and, inevitably, the resources available.

At least one university and one polytechnic have already brought their libraries, computing, and, in one case, educational technology services together in a common management structure, with an individual appointed with overall responsibility for the management and control of the service. By making the management of these inter-related services a central part of the institution's policy and decision-making processes, these seek to offer strong coordination and planning of central resource services within the context of the overall institutional mission. Furthermore, it offers possibilities for the development of integrated and inter-related services more relevant to the institution's future needs. It also removes the historical vertical divisions which have existed between services, particularly library and computing, and which are increasingly likely to become an impediment to the future development of information delivery systems for the whole institution. As a disadvantage, the model will be seen to have size and breadth of responsibilities, as well as the threat of increased bureaucracy, all of which must be countered by service delivery which is clearly focused on faculty and departmental requirements, and more specifically on the needs of students and staff. Such developments are relatively recent and it is, as yet, unclear how these services will be further developed and managed, though clearly in those institutions an opportunity has now been created, through a common structure of management and funding, to develop a more coordinated service. Given the wider implications of the electronic campus outlined above, these developments will be central to the overall institutional information strategy.

The disquiet which some might express about the size of such an organisation would suggest that the merger of large units such as libraries and computing services would be less welcome in some institutions and perhaps even considered impractical, if for no other reason than because of the span of responsibility they would place in one individual. Such institutions might choose to achieve a greater degree of coordination through a somewhat less defined faculty-like structure, which would still leave considerable autonomy to the managers of individual services, whilst at the same time ensuring a measure of coordinated development and planning both within the services and in a wider institutional context.

Many institutions of higher education believe coordination can best be achieved through a committee structure, though there is every indication that we are being encouraged to think of more direct systems of managerial control and responsibility, requirements which are not easily met by this particular model. It is a strategy which has, in other contexts, proved unsuccessful, resulting, as it so often does, in compromises which will progressively dilute the effectiveness of service provision. Whilst it might appear to offer opportunities for improving the coordination and planning of services, it is unlikely to enable difficult decisions to be taken.

Perhaps the greatest challenge lies in the obvious possibility now presented by the technology of devolving services to whatever sub-units of management may seem appropriate in an institution. It has already been indicated that networking and the availability of personal computers places greater control in the hands of individuals to determine access to and use of information, and utilisation of other facilities both within the institution and externally. Thus it is not surprising that some would argue for a greater say in the management and control of such services, an argument which receives added strength from the funding methodologies at present used in higher education. The opportunities these clearly present for buying in services would affect radically the concept of central management control and coordination. In the present context, it is not too difficult to counter such arguments, with factors such as resource duplication – both human and machine – non-standardisation and incompatibility of equipment though increasingly these will carry less weight in the context of the electronic campus. Those who argue for the devolved management of systems and services do, however, offer a real challenge to those who have responsibility for centrally managed services such as computing and library.

In considering the library/information services relationship with other support services, the focus has been largely on computing services, and others more directly concerned with the collection and management of information. Reference was made earlier, however, to educational technology units and it would be useful to return to that aspects of an institution's work for a moment. The diverse nature of such units is a problem in itself, though an attempt was made earlier to define precisely what was meant by the term. There is a natural caution among many academics about educational technology. Many are quick to remember the era of programmed learning, and the foolishness of those who advocated it as panacea. There is little doubt, however, that within the electronic campus new opportunities will exist. The range of delivery systems will increase, particularly for those who choose to study at a distance from the institution, and it seems probable that the educational technologist will be needed to help teachers prepare for new roles. The production of materials will also be of increasing importance, and training in systems such as desk-top publishing will further enhance the lecturer's ability to perform such functions from his own office desk or his home, whilst the whole question of integrating information skills into the curriculum has yet to be addressed. The ability to use network technologies to access video collections or databanks of other materials offers further opportunities to both the teacher and student to enhance both teaching and learning opportunities. New methods such as these, including video-based instruction, artificial intelligence systems for learning, and computer simulation, each have their implications for the overall information service, and libraries and other support services need to be acutely aware of an institution's educational processes and the likely impact information will have on teaching methods and student learning attitudes.

The focus thus far has been almost entirely on the academic work of the institution and on the traditional information providers. In any institution, there is, of course, an increasing number of other information providers, other than the library, including some outside the institution and, indeed, IT will mean an increase in these because of the ease and relatively low cost of distribution. Some, such as the registry and the finance office, have already been mentioned, but others are more directly the product of academic research interests or liaison with industrial and commercial concerns, which have led to the creation of specialist research institutes with appropriate information services operating in academic departments, often in isolation from central facilities. The departmental library is not new, particularly in the university sector, and no doubt its critics and protagonists will be in evidence in any representative group of academics. The computing equivalent also exists, arising out of a need to serve specialist research or teaching needs through software and hardware requirements which differ from the mainstream provision. Many such developments are inherently legitimate, even though they have apparently been developed independently of, and even in opposition to, centrally provided facilities. As a problem they are unlikely to go away totally, though in the context of the electronic campus their raison d'être is in need of re-examination. The opportunity to tailor information provision to the needs of departments, and even individuals, is one of the real bonuses of the new technology. The ability to make such information accessible almost anywhere removes the central argument for creating independent units. The emphasis is more that of distributing information rather than the collection and storage of information at any one point. However, the concept of scattered collections of information which can be linked together by a network also leads to the possibility of more effective use of an institution's distributed and isolated resources. Though a note of caution, since there is a price to pay for the establishment and linking of such resources which may well outstrip their realistic value. It has to be remembered, however, that arguments of economy of scale and ease of location and access, which have so often been used to justify the provision of central services, may no longer necessarily apply.

There is also the increasing clamour for management information systems (MIS). The need to improve services usually with less resources requires improvements in information and feedback to increase the effectiveness of management of all kinds of resources: teaching, financial, etc. This necessitates the rapid retrieval of information to support management decisions. Thus far such systems have, all too often, been developed in isolation from each other, often duplicating the collection of data, and, in their design, have taken little account of other institutional management needs. This has sometimes been forced on institutions by the need to design such systems to respond rapidly to external bodies, a requirement which has often prevented the careful assessment of the broader context of such systems, and the relationship between internal and external requirements. In some instances, such systems must of necessity work with highly confidential or even sensitive information, and this must be respected, but they often draw on data and produce data which in the context of the wider information environment could be useful to others. The whole question of security of information within a complex information network is one which must be addressed quite separately from this paper. Other opportunities exist, of course, in the information environment: electronic mail, viewdata, internal databases, all have their potential. Librarians and computing specialists are already familiar with such applications, and are able to bring their respective skills to the enhancement of services. Unfortunately, independent services are still developed by well-meaning individuals who are generally unaware of access to other information sources, and all too often they do little more than reinvent the wheel.

Reference was made earlier to the concept of central facilities as against distributed resources, both in the context of the management of computing systems and the remote location of information sources. Because of the nature of the technology, it would be simple to suggest that within the electronic campus many of the issues associated with these problems can be solved, and to some extent that is correct if the institution develops an overall information strategy which clearly defines the roles of the constituent parts. Hitherto, arguments for devolving services and facilities have centred around control and access, whilst those for centralisation focus on economies of scale, the unnecessary duplication of expensive resources, and general access. Networking has, indeed, the power to offer the possibility of providing access to information in whatever form simply through the intermediary of a computer terminal, whilst remotely held collections of materials are less problematic, provided they form part of the total information resources of the institution and can be accessed via the network. But this is rather too simplistic a model. The reality is that even in the electronic campus it will still be necessary to cope with the problem of managing distributed systems.

Many polytechnic and some university librarians would argue that they have been forced to operate in this way for some considerable time in running site libraries, and apart from obvious disadvantages such as resource duplication, and staff isolation, they would probably argue that they allowed the development of services which are more clearly focused on the needs of individual faculties and departments within the context of the overall service. In a similar fashion computing managers have seen a rapid translation from the centralised system to distributed processing. In many cases this has been accompanied by the development of appropriate communication systems, linking some elements together, or at the very least back to the central system. It has, however, made significantly different demands on staff support both for hardware and for software. In some institutions strong central policy has dictated the nature of computing developments by prescribing particular kinds of hardware and software with a view to easing the burden on staff faced with providing support for an increasing complexity of systems. In some others, however, there has been a greater degree of laissez faire, which has resulted either in disappointment when the central service has been unable to support the developments, or in a greater degree of self-sufficiency on the part of lecturing staff faced with the need to utilise the resources for teaching and research. The underlying problem is likely to be less one of location than of control, and the role of institution-wide services, as opposed to other institutional sub-groups, must be clearly defined. Central management of the services has the advantage of providing an overall scheme of control, though it will always have to balance this against the needs of individual sub-groups within an institution. For the service staff themselves, their participation as part of an institutional service reduces professional isolation, and allows them to develop their particular part of the service within the context of the wider institutional service. Though part of a central service, experience suggests that they also act as powerful advocates on behalf of their faculty/department/unit within the development of the overall service, informed as they should be about academic developments and plans, and in so doing they can be identified as much with the sub-unit as they are with the central service.

In addressing the organisational implications of the electronic campus, it is necessary to recognise that we are no longer concerned with individual services, such as libraries, computing centres, or educational technology units, but with the institution as a whole. The technology and its consequences has the power to pervade every aspect of an institution's work, and for that reason it is a central requirement to evolve an information strategy, which clearly defines the roles of the contributing elements within the structure and sets the parameters within which other information-based developments take place. Whilst this will be particularly important for libraries and computing centres, many of whose roles are converging, it will also apply to other areas of the institution's academic and administrative processes. Its absence will result in an unproductive anarchy of development in which individual systems and schemes will be developed, incompatible with the needs of the institution. The definition of the relationship between the central services and other resourcing agents will be pivotal to the strategy, as will be the structure for their management. The particular organisational model chosen to effect this, however, is likely to depend on a variety of local variables. The priorities which will need to be set by the management of these new services are challenging, as is the need to develop new services. For those working in the services, there should be little cause for concern. There are those who preach the end of libraries, even though the book and its reader is still one of the most powerful information processing mediums available. Book collections will form part of the total information for a long time to come. For some institutions, the book-based library will remain their most important resource, whilst for others they will be forced to concentrate more on access to information than on the storage of knowledge. The challenges for the library and information professions are immense. For the computing specialists there are whole new areas of support at all levels of the technology, as well as in the increasingly important communication technologies, and the need to address the multifarious demands of lecturers and students wishing to harness the power of the technology in their studies, teaching and research. For the teacher, researcher, manager and administrator, the boundaries are unlimited but also unpredictable. Such demands will require greater flexibility, and an even clearer understanding of the educational process on the part of all those involved in the provision of information services.

References

[1] McLuhan, M. *Understanding Media: the Extensions of Man.* 1964.

[2] Shaughnessy, T. W. Technology and the structure of libraries. *Libri,* 32(2), 1982.

[3] McLean, N. IT82: a polytechnic response - opening remarks. *Aslib Proceedings,* 34(10), October, 1982.

[4] Brindley, L. J. The wired-up campus and the future of the information service. *The Newsletter of the Library Association Information Technology Group,* 15, January, 1988.

Case Study: Southampton University

Bernard Naylor, *Southampton University*

Independence of thought, and, by implication, independence of initiative are special hallmarks of the university environment. It is an environment in which a strategy is more likely to command support if it coalesces within the community than if it is imposed, by analogy with a corporate business enterprise, through action imposed from the top. The penetration of the Southampton University academic community by electronic technology and the formation of an information strategy have been important parts of a process in which separate strands of development are, in due course, perceived to have essential common elements, requiring that they be brought together into a coherent programme and in which some of the diverse members of the academic community realise that a university information strategy is something which needs to be devised and to which they ought to give their commitment. This description of the Southampton experience to date will not systematically examine the topics mentioned in the supporting material for the conference but it will nevertheless provide a good exploration of them in a particular environment.

The beginning of the story can be traced to an initiative in the field of word processing taken by the University in 1978. Already a number of departments were giving a lead by introducing early examples of word processing equipment, but there was quite a widespread feeling that many departments were being forced to settle for second best because of the inadequacy of the packages then available. The feeling was strongest on the science side where the most complex parts of research papers (for example mathematical equations or biochemical formulae) could not be handled by the then available packages. On the humanities side, too, departments were asking why a full range of fonts, such as Greek, Russian or even Old English, could not be handled more effectively and more simply than the vendors of the standard commercial packages were inclined to say they could. A Working Group on Word Processing Equipment, later called the Advisory Group on Information Handling, was established and the Southern Universities Organisation and Methods Unit, now the Southern Universities Management Services Unit, was asked to carry out an investigation of available technology and to see whether a better product could not be teased out of the suppliers.

The outcome of this initiative was the adoption by the University of the Compucorp word processing package during the 1982-3 session. It included both hardware and software in a single deal, and provided for two levels, one capable of providing most if not all that the critics of the other systems were asking for, and the other, a more simple level, which was satisfactory for those departments wanting more straightforward facilities. The development owed much to special work carried out on the software in Southampton University, notably by Dr Graham Thomas of the Electronics Department, and it was written up in *The Times Higher Education Supplement*. Between thirty and forty screens were introduced across the University. The package was also adopted by some other universities.

Even as this work was coming to fruition, it was clear that the technology was developing so quickly as to outstrip what was being done. In particular, the rapid increase in the number of low cost word processors becoming available convinced many departments that they did not need the expensive option of the Compucorp system. The Advisory Group on Information Handling was associated in many people's minds with introducing a Rolls-Royce solution (albeit a successful one) to some very difficult problems and at the same time was seen as being indifferent to the everyday needs of many secretaries across the campus. And not only secretaries, because, stimulated partly by the reduction in secretarial support following the 1981 cuts, and partly by their own appetite for hands-on experience, increasing numbers of academic and other staff were wanting access to word processors too.

In those early days, it was already clear that there could be no question of imposing a single choice of equipment on the whole University. Southampton University's strong history of budgetary devolution precluded that. (When the Advisory Group turned its attention to the question of low-cost packages, it started by investigating what was already in use in the University, in order to build on whatever accidental consensus there might already be.) However, four factors were even then identified as contributing towards greater standardisation. These were:

- Central negotiation of favourable bulk purchase terms for preferred equipment.

- Central support of maintenance (by staff of the University Computing Service) for preferred equipment at lower cost that could be provided by the manufacturers or their commercial agents.

- Central provision of training and continuing user support for users of preferred equipment.

- Preference for preferred equipment in any arrangements for connection to a University network.

Despite all the subsequent developments yet to be outlined, those remain the principal planks of our efforts towards a common policy. The carrot is mightier than the stick.

The Director of the Computing Service and the University Librarian were both early members of the Advisory Group on Information Handling, having both expressed a strong interest in likely developments. Although initial efforts did concentrate on word processing, these two senior officers of the University, together with a third, the Director of the Teaching Media Department (responsible, among other things, for the use of technology in support of teaching), were conscious that their respective departments were converging on a common area of potential service development which was opening up because of advances in IT . They had started to meet informally and on an irregular basis to compare notes on this topic, and to establish a modus vivendi in particular instances requiring an urgent response. Their personal relations were positive and strong but they were the first to point out that this could have adverse consequences for the vigorous pursuit of possible initiatives; any individualistic entrepreneurial spirit was just as likely to be tempered by a wish to give priority to maintaining good relations with a colleague who might also see some particular opportunity as equally appropriate to his own department. They also pointed out that Southampton University's strong system of budgetary devolution made it more difficult to launch initiatives which could not be exclusively assigned to one of the three service departments, particularly as there was no agreed basis for transferring costs as there was, for example, for service teaching. At the early stage, their views did not carry the conviction which a gradually cumulating supply of examples eventually provided, but they did continually urge on the Advisory Group the importance of closer relations between their three departments if they were to optimise their contribution to the academic development of the University.

As well as embarking on a specific project, the introduction of advanced word processing, and being asked to note an important new theme of interdepartmental collaboration, the Advisory Group also established status as a consultative body for other developments which it felt, or other people felt, related to its purpose. So, when the University replaced its main telephone exchange in 1984, the Advisory Group was consulted. When the Library decided to introduce the University's first fax station (a possibility the Group had previously canvassed across the University but on which it had met widespread indifference) the Group was kept informed. When staff changes provided the opportunity for a further review of message transmission, the Group promoted a change which saw the transfer of both the fax station and the University main telex station (also till then in the Library) to the Computing Service, which it was felt had the special technical skills needed for future development towards a decentralised pattern of operation. Another important aspect of these developments was that they left no doubt that the impact of the Group must extend right into the area of the professional administration as well as into the teaching departments.

Although the Advisory Group had been active for a number of years and been involved in several initiatives, by 1986 it was still not seen as having a central role in the University. The arrival of a new Vice-Chancellor was a suitable moment to take stock of the general pace of technological advance. From the beginning of the 1986-7 session, Dr Higginson himself took over as Chairman of the Group (now renamed the Information Services Advisory Group) and this projected it into the centre of the University's affairs.

In the last two years, the Group's vision of the future has sharpened noticeably and now focuses on the following basic premises:

- Accessing and processing information is at the heart of most university activity.

- The vdu screen will be a fundamental tool of the future for those needing to access and process information.

- Those in the University needing to access and process information through a vdu screen should be able to access all they want from a single screen whether it be administrative data (such as student registration or financial information) or academic data (library files or other databases). The one screen should also admit them to computing facilities appropriate to their academic speciality, and should enable them to manipulate information, and to create new information, both administrative and academic.

- The single vdu screen, depending on its location, will have to serve many different functions. It will have to be as friendly to the Grade 2 secretary in the Registry as to the Dean of the Arts Faculty, or for that matter the Professor of Electronics. The availability of different levels of operating complexity, making different assumptions about the competence of the screen operator, is implied.

Of course, these premises represent an ideal and the chances of achieving it completely at an early stage are not strong. The University has a well developed vision, but little or no plan. However, the vision marks out the path of development well into the future and future initiatives can be shaped and judged in terms of the contribution they make to the practical programme we shall need to carry us along our development path.

I have already said that our initiative is partly seen as a response to specific challenges which seem to demand that we cut across the boundaries of existing activities. Here are four practical examples currently in process.

First, we need to arrange for interactive computing to be projected by video in our lecture theatres. At present the expertise in and budgetary responsibility for interactive computing lies with the Computing Service while the Teaching Media Department takes responsibility for the exploitation of video in the lecture theatres. Specialists in these two areas of expertise must have the maximum encouragement to work together on new developments. Those responsible for the administration of each service and for its finances must be encouraged to put the proper arrangements in place to secure the future of new developments, not only in the planning stage but also when they are fully operational.

Second, we need to consider how we are to provide access to information (for example, about materials) for engineering students working in computer-aided design workshops. Some of this material is available in printed form, some in microfiche, some as an online database, and soon no doubt some will be available on CD-ROM, if it is not already available in that format. We need to clear our minds on a number of questions. For example, is this a laboratory or workshop facility or is it really a library facility? Will we want to access the machine-readable databases using online searching over

PSS and IPSS in the mode now well-established in the library or will we want to buy the database in and mount it on the Computing Service's mainframe? The answer may be determined by economic considerations, but, whatever the answer is, it has awkward budgetary implications in our present structure. If we buy the database, do we have any technical preference as between CD-ROM (probably available in the Library or the department) and mounting the database on the University mainframe? There is clearly a substantial risk of providing a muddled and unevenly developed service with varied rules and methods of access and possibly a varied financial framework. (There is a well-established tradition of charging for online services but not for the use of the mainframe or the library's own stock.) An integrated service may be better able to give a fully coherent response.

Third, by exploiting the flexibility of computer-controlled interactive video, there is great potential for the development of personal learning materials in the form of multi-faceted and multi-level packages. At present, there are very few instances world-wide of packages which fully exploit the scope of the technologies. (I know of only two, one on the terracotta Chinese warriors, the other on the Brazilian artist, Portinari.) They are bound to become more common in the future even though at present the capital investment required for their creation looks formidable. Who will take responsibility for such services, the library with its long tradition of supporting personal self-motivated learning, the Computing Service with its high expertise in computer applications, or the Teaching Media Department with its deep knowledge of the uses of video in education? We must also not lose sight of the fact that research and development in an electronics or computing science department may be the essential precursor of a practical service.

Fourth, the University (or rather the Computing Service and the Library in collaboration) has recently invested in the advanced OCR capabilities of the Kurzweil machine. At this stage, it is seen as having great importance for rapid exploitation of the research potential locked up in the (mainly typewritten) Mountbatten archive. It is also seen as an important adjunct to the History Department in its rapid build-up of the teaching potential implicit in the HIDES (HIstorical Documents Expert System) Project. But it may well also play a crucial role in helping the University build administrative machine-readable files, where the sheer size of the problem of encoding backfiles (for example of committee minutes and papers) would otherwise look insoluble.

In this vision of the screen-focused working environment, the Administration clearly ought to have an important place. In the past, the emphasis in administration has been on the efficient processing of data. In the end, we all agree to give higher priority to paying salaries or registering students than to opening up access to information about payroll costs or student details. The advance of the technology is cheapening the marginal cost of adding information access to the data-processing function. A close study of the requirements for access to information by a wide range of University staff is now being launched, whether they be staff who are hired expressly to process administrative data or staff who process it as a more or less disagreeable second priority to their first priority academic role.

The chief problem in the administrative sector is deciding where to draw the boundaries. The case for bringing the telephone exchange within the traditional Computing Service is now almost incontestable. It is more a matter of choosing the strategic moment. Campus printing facilities are a slightly less obvious case, but one that is likely to get stronger in the very near future. Likely developments in the interface between keyboarding and rapid copying, developments which will eliminate the need to print out an intermediate 'master' copy, will take the process even further. The gradual change in the format and use of the traditional student registration card, to make it double as a library card, with machine-readable data encoded, and then to find further use as a computing access card, is already with us, but the management of card issue is still driven by the registration function. In due course, the card may also become essential for access to campus buildings as security becomes an increasingly important requirement and technological answers are sought. However, administrative functions themselves must clearly continue to be distinguished from, and not subordinated to, the data handling function. The technology is opening a discussion about the boundaries, about the where and the how of this distinction.

If the fullest benefits are to be derived from the technology, the investment has to be long-term. As a result, long-term questions about the future role of the institution have to be considered in an earlier timescale. One example is the likely development of the pattern of higher education over the next two decades. In one scenario, Southampton University may emerge as the leading institution in a federation of higher education sector institutions in the Solent hinterland. If this is to happen, our information transfer links require early thought. Another open question is how far and in what way the University's role will develop in the field of adult and continuing education. Methods of information transfer (remote lectures 'attended' through video links?) could play a crucial role. A third question concerns the role of the University as a centre of broad-ranging and high-level expertise, combined with an experienced and high-performance research capability. If local enterprises are to make the kind of use of our capabilities which their needs and our ambitions indicate they should, our information infrastructure will have to play a crucial role.

That is a lot of speculation for what is billed as 'a case study'. An important and pragmatic first step is to lay the physical network infrastructure which will carry machine-readable information round our community. This project has now been set in motion by a university decision to commit the necessary initial resources at a time when any form of exceptional capital expenditure is extremely difficult to achieve in the university environment. Special UGC funding would be an immense fillip and would almost certainly enable us to compress the investment period and start to deliver the benefits sooner. The project requires a major exercise in investigating the expectations of potential users and the capabilities of potential information providers. It is likely to have a considerable educational effect in itself and to stimulate further vigorous thinking in many quarters about our impending 'information culture'.

Although rightly presented as a major new initiative, it is equally fair to characterise the network project rather differently. The campus is currently served by a network based on Gandalf technology. This and the Campus Packet Switching Exchange (CPSE) are both reaching the limits of their capacity. The existing provision will be saturated by about mid-1990, according to current projections. It is therefore crucial for the University to open up a development path if departments are not to be denied further connections to campus facilities. The Network Project will secure that development path. If the University can be brought to understand this view of an admittedly expensive development, they may find it more palatable, not least because it is the indispensable complement to the steady and cumulating investment in peripheral devices which we know they are making in the same timescale. Most of the illustrations of the increasing overlap between the Library, the Computing Service and the Teaching Media Department have arisen naturally and unavoidably as enthusiastic professionals have tried to extend the range of services they provide. It is now additionally envisaged that bringing the three services closer together could provide an opportunity to foster a climate in which innovation through interaction is more likely to emerge. If new forms of service are being derived from a mixing of the best in the traditions of the three departments, perhaps the staff of the three services should start to work across the traditional departmental boundaries. In the programme now being envisaged, staff from each of the three services will get the opportunity to experience the working environment of the other services and it is hoped that this will help to broaden their horizons and their imaginations about the possibilities for service development. It is hoped to encourage this interaction at all levels of the staff complement and in a manner appropriate to the responsibilities and the potential of the staff. At the most senior level, it is hoped that a corporate service culture will take shape from which will emerge the future pattern of provision.

Changes in organisational structure look like the inevitable accompaniment to this process and changes of that kind are indeed being implemented. With effect from 1 August 1988, the University Librarian has been additionally appointed Coordinator of Information Services for a term of five years with a mandate to promote greater collaboration among the three services. The Director of the Computing Service has recently retired and serious thought has been given to the management structure which will be most appropriate for his successor in the changing environment. A strong case is felt to exist for making the Coordinator the single reporting point between the services and the Vice-Chancellor. The present writer is clear that, whatever the structure adopted, the attitude of the leaders of the three departments towards the implications of, and the opportunities afforded by, technical convergence are of the utmost importance.

The University's committee structure is also being reviewed to take account of these changes. The Information Services Advisory Committee, previously floating free, is now being linked more closely into a structure in which the Computing Service Committee, the Library Committee and the Teaching Media Committee continue to play their former role yet are being required to relate actively with an over-arching body.

As far as funding is concerned, no changes have so far been made. It is accepted that the University community will be watching closely for any signs that one of the activities (inevitably their favourite) is being surreptitiously or even flagrantly milked in the interests of one or both of the others. But identifying and freeing funds for future developments will be important. The University has its own well established procedure (the 'Project Fund') for encouraging innovation, and there is no reason why this should not be seen as a potential source. But even while retaining the integrity of the three activities it may be possible to identify small amounts of money which can be freed. It is hoped soon to have a management study of the non-specialist areas of each of the three departments to see whether there is scope for organising differently such activities as recruitment, staff induction and training, accounts control, etc. A measure of bet-hedging can clearly be detected in these arrangements, and there are sound reasons for that. The book and the periodical seem to have some life left in them yet, the manuscript still more so. 'Number crunching' in the Science Faculty will not disappear in the near future. Blackboards, slides, and overhead projectors will probably still be heavily used by the end of the century and beyond. Our current publicity continues to lay strong emphasis on the viability and value of the different service traditions of the three service departments. Featureless uniformity is not the goal. In any process aimed at optimising the take up of new technology, care must be taken to safeguard the enduringly useful elements of the old technologies as well. Perhaps those elements will predominate for many years to come. We are not so confident of the pace of future development that we are prepared to make final decisions now on those points.

In this context, it is not easy to respond directly to the query about 'the future place of the library'. Libraries themselves have changed remarkably in the last thirty years and the process of change is accelerating. Within that period, services which are now commonplace have been seen as bastard intruders on a legitimate and settled service tradition. The Director of the Computing Service and I have often spoken of the future gradual erosion of the boundaries of our respective bailiwicks. In inviting me to accept the role of Coordinator of Information Services, the Vice-Chancellor said that he saw it not as a new and different role from the one I had exercised as University Librarian, but the natural extension of it. However, flexibility is all, at this stage. In five years time, it could be decided that the innovation has not proved itself and that the status quo ante should be restored, or we may decide that the process of integration of the three services (plus, quite likely, some additional ancillary elements which are now part of the Administration) has grown to the extent that it cannot and should not be reversed but should continue or be carried even further.

Case Study: Aston University

Lynne Brindley, *Aston University*

Introduction

This case study focuses on the position of the Library and Information Services at Aston University. It is set in the context of the overall University strategy and in particular Aston's commitment to use of information technology across all activities.

Aston is a technological university whose ethos derives from its commitment to serve the needs of society, particularly industry, commerce and public service. Its academic disciplines and programmes are chosen for their evident relevance to this outside world and in that sense even its Modern Languages Department is 'technological' in orientation by concentrating, not on literature, but on the modern history, politics and socio-economics of the relevant country, combined with its language. The University has three faculties: Engineering, Science, and Management and Modern Languages, with a student population of some 4000.

University strategy

Since the major cuts of July 1981, when Aston took a 31% drop in its recurrent grant, the University has undertaken a comprehensive restructuring programme. This has identified long-term objectives and the most effective means of achieving them. It has followed a consistent quality-driven, demand-led strategy through the restructuring of its academic programmes, merger or closure of half of its departments, and departure of half of its academic and non-academic staff. It has rebuilt its library and computing infrastructure, and is well advanced in a physical restructuring programme which will relocate nearly all of its departments in refurbished accommodation and re-landscape the entire campus.

In working towards its aims the University's first consideration has always been to balance its budget and to live within its diminishing means. The restructuring of faculties and departments is now largely complete. All academic programmes have been revamped and show marked improvement in their attractiveness to highly-qualified UCCA candidates, with an overall average A-level points score of 11.6 (well within the top third of all UK universities). In research, particular emphasis has been placed on the formation of groups in areas where they can build upon existing strengths to address high-priority topics. A large number of professorial appointments are in progress to improve leadership in key research areas, but it will be some time before this aspect of planning comes to full fruition. It is also an important element in Aston's strategy to strengthen academically challenging links with industry and commerce, and to contribute to the economic regeneration of the West Midlands. The Aston Science Park is flourishing and now employs some 500 people, and the West Midlands Technology Transfer Centre, housed on campus, is well underway in promoting technology awareness and facilitating access to research expertise in higher education in the region.

Information technology strategy

A central and distinctive part of the University's strategy is a commitment to the use of IT across all its activities. Despite financial constraints, Aston has been investing significantly of its own resources to build up a powerful IT infrastructure to support the entire range of its teaching, research and administrative programmes. In 1982, for example, an integrated library system was implemented, giving Aston early experience of automating all its library processes. By 1984 Aston had established a unique Centre of Extension Education based around the use of video methods of instruction. Three lecture theatres and associated editing facilities provide an in-house production facility of some 2500 broadcast hours of video each year, used live for student lectures and in distance learning mode for updating professionals and managers in industry.

More recently, and with support from the Computer Board, the University's central computing facilities were upgraded to provide access to some £2 million of DEC equipment for research and advanced teaching. Most departments have their own computing laboratories, for such activities as computer-aided design work, through to sophisticated business simulation games for management students. The University has also been innovative in its introduction of office automation. There is a large community of electronic mail users and an ever-increasing presence of microcomputers, now approaching 1000, and widely used for word processing, spreadsheets, and database facilities, at the desks of academics and administrators alike.

The culmination of this IT strategy is a recently announced £4 million project, Project ACCENT, to install a broadband, OSI local area network spanning the entire campus and wiring up each room with service points for both data and video. This project is being supported financially by both the DTI and the UGC, and is the most technologically advanced LAN currently planned for Europe. It is the first DTI Demonstrator Project for OSI and will be a case study for the UGC in its evaluation of network models for the UK university system. A significant part of the project will be the demonstration of networked library and information services including OSI protocols, described further below.

The University's continuing commitment to an advanced IT strategy was expressed in the Vice-Chancellor's Annual Report of 1986-87, which states in its prescription for Aston's future:

> Aston must continue to improve its IT infrastructure, particularly by provision of a campus-wide local area network, and maintain its leading position among British universities in information services and computing. Special emphasis must be given to knowledge-based computing.

Library and information services strategy

The University's overall strategy and its commitment to a strong IT infrastructure have been outlined to give a picture of the environment within which the Library and Information Services (LIS) operates. Key relevant characteristics are the very fast pace of change and restructuring, the need for continuing change, the applied nature of the academic programmes and the emphasis on widespread use of information and IT . It was rightly decided that the model of a traditional, collection-focused university library would be inappropriate and indeed unachievable. So what is the strategy for the LIS?

In 1985-86 a fundamental review of the operations of the University Library was undertaken, the appointment of a new Director of Library and Information Services was made, and a forward strategy and model for services into the 1990s was developed. The Library had the advantage at that time of being well automated, including the use of external bibliographic services. It shared with other younger institutions the lack of significant historical collections, both in depth and breadth.

Taking this into account, together with the size and subject orientation of the academic programmes, and our view of longer-term trends in electronic publishing, we are choosing a rather distinctive approach. All opportunities are being taken to develop the LIS as a proactive information service of the kind more usually associated with industrial and special libraries than with academic libraries. This is particularly true in our support of research, and increasingly true in support of advanced project work in undergraduate programmes. We do not have the benefit of large research collections but this has advantages in that it enables us to move more easily and quickly to an information-led strategy, relying on access to provide relevant research support in fast-moving areas. These priorities are reflected in LIS resource distribution, for example, where we spend minimally on binding and preservation, while spending three times as much on external document supply services and online database searching.

LIS service model

The model being followed is characterised by the following:

- Service orientation. All effort is made to encourage full use of the LIS, to provide visible, tailored services to support particular user groups, and as many resources as possible are put into front-line activities.

- Collection development to serve current needs. The collection is not being developed against some unknown future, but to serve immediate needs of teaching and research. Weeding is as important as collecting! The collection matches current academic priorities and resources are selectively distributed towards purchasing in depth in areas of particular strength at research level, and in relation to demand and usage at teaching level.

- Cataloguing to serve basic bibliographic needs. Some 70% of cataloguing records are purchased from external sources, and most processing work is done at a para-professional or clerical level.

- Rapid and comprehensive access to other sources. The core collection is supplemented by unrationed document supply services from other sources. Requests are carefully monitored to see if purchase of the material, particularly a serial title, is justified.

- Proactive information services. A team of five information specialists attached to faculties leads an extensive programme of information services, ranging from information skills programmes at all levels, online searching of databases and databanks, end-user searching services with advisory support, to current awareness and alerting services.

- Exploitation of IT . In all these activities cost-effective use of IT is pursued as vigorously as possible.

To support these developments a particular management framework is being followed. Continued emphasis is given to links with academic staff and close relationships with changing academic programmes and priorities. This has been both essential and difficult over the past few years of rapid change. The service-based strategy requires a high visibility and promotion of services on offer, and considerable attention is paid to the creation of a greater awareness of what the LIS can offer and how it fits in academic programmes. Staff development at all levels is a key feature to ensure full contribution to this rapidly changing environment. Priority is being given to the development of IT, management and customer relations skills.

Strategic implications

This strategy is being followed with some success in establishing an image and institutional role for the LIS associated with support of both traditional and electronic information provision. It is the combination of Aston's 'electronic campus' environment, including the expectations of students and staff, combined with the availability of a range of electronic products and services in Aston's central academic disciplines, that make the LIS strategy achievable.

Quite deliberately the LIS is an active participant in exploiting the wider computing facilities available on campus. We use electronic mail as part of service provision – for the delivery of online search results to the personal computer of the academic and the relaying of relevant fragments of information as part of a current awareness profile. We are major users of the University's database and information retrieval software mounted on the mainframe, for the creation of LIS training files and the creation of in-house databases. Additionally we provide supervision for a regular flow of MSc IT student projects on LIS related topics, and some departments are keen for us to develop computer appreciation programmes for their students, to complement information skills programmes.

Student expectation of the LIS is high, as is their level of IT literacy. They are largely enthusiastic (and perhaps too uncritical) supporters of all services electronic. This year has seen the installation, with UGC Library Networking Initiative resources, of a 12-workstation training facility. We will be running programmes to ensure a full awareness and use by all Aston students of relevant electronic information sources in their subject areas, in addition to learning to exploit traditional materials.

Aston's LAN project, which has already been mentioned, gives the next opportunity for a major step forward in electronic information service provision. These plans have been described in detail elsewhere [1]. They enable us to fulfil more fully than before the philosophy of the electronic library, through the delivery of a far wider range of services to the academic's or student's desk. Networked access to the catalogue will be available more widely, with the possibility of downloading and editing reading lists and bibliographies at the desk. Users will be able to enquire, place reservations, and make renewals of library stock without having to visit the Library building. Books and documents will be ordered through the distributed mail service. The demonstration of OSI protocols will facilitate international bibliographic record transfer. Our support of online information searching will be possible over the network, providing a remote classroom facility via a video channel. It is envisaged that requests for interlibrary loans will be sent over the network from users' desks with possible delivery via fax back around the network, for local printing or loading into the personal computer, copyright permitting!

Organisational change

The LIS strategy has brought with it organisational change resulting in a significant redistribution of professional resources within the same overall complement, from the backroom processing functions into a newly created Information Services Division of six staff. Only three key professionals are left managing and developing policy in the technical processing areas, within which most activity is undertaken by clerical staff under supervision. The LIS also seeks to work closely with staff from the Computing Service, as our interests begin to converge. On a wider front, in March 1987 the Director of LIS was appointed as the University's first Pro-Vice-Chancellor for Information Technology, in addition to her LIS responsibilities. This post has University-wide responsibility for the development of IT strategy for academic and administrative matters.

Summary of wider issues

Aston has a clear academic and IT strategy for the University. Within this context it has been appropriate to develop a Library and Information Service strategy which is information-focused and fully exploits IT and an increasing range of electronic products and services. This strategy is fully supported in the University, but it has particular implications. It requires staff with a high level of IT skills; it brings rapid and continuing change; a rolling investment in IT requires high levels of capital expenditure; electronic products and services are at present expensive and often cannot substitute for more traditional printed materials. An access strategy is only really practical through dependency on the British Library Document Supply Centre and assumes the continuation of an effective and affordable service from that source. These issues will be explored further in the presentation of the case study.

References

[1] Brindley, L. J. Planning for library and information services over a campus-wide network. *Netlink*, 3, May 1987, 4-10.

Case Study: Edinburgh University

Brenda Moon, *Edinburgh University*

All the libraries about which we are hearing today, whether in metropolitan universities, technological universities, large old universities such as Edinburgh, or polytechnics, support research to a greater or lesser degree, and I suspect that the key issues are very much the same for them all, though they may not have the same priorities. I should like to highlight three which are taxing us in Edinburgh today, and are likely to remain key issues for the next few years; they are communications, standards, and access.

Communications have been a vital element in Edinburgh University's computing policy from the beginning, since the teaching and research of the eight faculties is dispersed over several square miles of the city. The Edinburgh Multi-Access System (EMAS) developed by the Computing Service in the early days has served the academic community well for many years, and still provides not least an efficient electronic mail service, though it is by no means the only operating system in use in the University.

In recent years faculties and departments have increasingly acquired their own computers, chiefly for research. The Library expects shortly to be using a machine in the Department of Geography and the CARTONET software developed in the Department for the graphic and descriptive cataloguing of its map collection. For the most part, however, the Library turns next after its own system to one of the mainframes maintained by the Computing Service, mounting on it an information service for network users. The number of access points on the University network (EDNET) has grown rapidly during the eighties. There are now over two thousand outlets, and this number could double within the next decade.

The University Library and the Management Information Service (a department of the Secretary's office, serving the administrative needs of the University) have also installed their own systems selected to meet current housekeeping needs, but not fully integrated with the systems adopted by the Computing Service, so that transmitting data from one host to another still presents problems. The University is currently planning its strategy for the 1990s, and one of the prime objectives will be to ensure that both Library and Management Information Service systems are fully compatible with the University's chosen communications network, when that is decided. The Computing Service is fully committed to the Joint Network Team (JNT) and Computer Board software standards, and in due course to the use of International Standards Organisation (ISO) protocols as these emerge. The Library is also committed to the adoption of the ISO Open Systems Interconnection protocols. At present its GEAC computer system is a host on the University's X.25 network. When the Library automation programme was initiated in 1983 there were three objectives: to automate housekeeping routines on all library sites, to distribute library information over the University network, and to create a bibliographic database which would record all its holdings. The continuation of this programme is a key element in the University's academic plan, for which it has earmarked resources until 1990. For the creation of the database, involving the retrospective conversion of the catalogues, the Library has also received massive support from the Manpower Services Commission under its Community Programme.

All sections of the Library, which serves the eight faculties on eight major and seven minor sites and maintains small collections in a number of other departments, are now linked to the Library's GEAC computer, and current acquisitions in all fields except law and music are catalogued by computer. The bibliographic database now records over half a million volumes including most of the modern monograph collections in science, medicine, arts and social sciences. A copy of the database is mounted on one of the Computing Service mainframes, partly as a security measure, partly to diffuse traffic.

The automation of lending routines in the Main Library in particular has brought almost a doubling of borrowing activity since the automation programme began, and although some of this increase may be due to a reduction in the maximum loan period allowed, it is thought to be largely due to improved control and to the information provided online on the availability of the books readers seek. There are currently over 23 000 registered users of the Library's services.

Now for the first time the holdings of all sections of the Library are represented in one database, and this has resulted in changing patterns of use. Readers no longer confine themselves so readily to their nearest collection. A survey has shown that ten per cent of the readers in the central Medical Library are from the Science Faculty site two miles away. The collections are being more fully and more diversely exploited.

In the University at large the move to desk-top computing has been marked over the past five years and there is no evidence that the trend is weakening. Personal computers and more powerful workstations are now in widespread use by academic staff and research students, but the day is still some way off when every researcher will have a personal computer on his desk. Hardware and software must be shared, and the Library plays a part in providing access. The 'public terminal room' in the Main Library has become a 'microshop' where staff and students can obtain advice and help from the Computing Service on systems appropriate to their needs. The Medical Library will soon be home to a Faculty of Medicine 'microlab' designed primarily for tuition but available for individual use when not otherwise occupied.

Collaboration between the Library and the Computing Service has been close from the start of the Library automation programme, and is now seen as a vital element in the University's academic plan, which aims to provide an integrated information service to the academic community. The Director of the Computing Service and the Librarian are joined by the Director of Management Information in regular meetings to discuss matters of common concern. Collaboration with the Computing Service will be even easier when the user support staff of the Computing Service move into the Main Library during the coming year. A particular instance of collaboration is the work done jointly by the Library and the Data Library Service, a unit within the Computing Service, on the cataloguing of computer files.

A research library will always have, however, a special role in supporting research, which a computing service does not share: it maintains collections. It must preserve the research of the past, the output of the pre-electronic age, and lay down stocks for the future. It must keep a good cellar. The book and the microfiche are still economic and reliable ways of archiving information. A computing service is primarily concerned with transmitting information; in spite of the huge capacity of their machines, most have never acquired the collecting habit.

It was a recognition of the central importance of the collections, especially for research in the humanities, that made the retrospective conversion of the catalogues a vital element in the Library's programme from the start. The creation of the database is by far the most costly element in that programme. The installation of hardware and software throughout the Library network and the linking of the Library system to the Computing Service network will have

100

involved a capital expenditure of about £1 million by 1990; the creation of a database covering only part of the collections will have cost approximately £2 million. The cost of recording the remaining collections – notably the special collections of early books and manuscripts which constitute about 12% of the whole – has not yet been estimated. Estimates are complex, for some of these materials have never been adequately catalogued before.

The Library must constantly seek more cost-effective ways of conducting this huge task. It has resisted the temptation to adopt other than the national standards established by the British Library because it believes that its collections are of national, and indeed international, significance for research. The development of standards is as much a key issue for the Library as it is for the Computing Service. The cost of adhering not simply to institutional standards but to the somewhat irksome AACR2 and UKMarc formulae is high, but the Library firmly believes that the cost of not doing so will be higher in the long run. This conviction was strengthened a year ago when a collection of five thousand books was transferred, along with teaching and research in the subject, from another university. The records, though in machine-readable form, could not be merged because different standards had been adopted. Conversion from one standard to another – even from LCMarc to UKMarc – costs money. If problems of format are serious within the library community, how much more are problems to be expected in standardising information handling and document transmission throughout a university, even more throughout the academic community at large. No research library is an island, and collaboration with others is vital both for academic and for economic reasons. Edinburgh is therefore an eager participant in the programme on which the Consortium of University Research Libraries (CURL) embarked last year, with strong support from the UGC, for the creation of a database of its members' holdings. Their records are not merged, though held in one file, with a joint index, on an Amdahl computer at Manchester University. CURL is committed to AACR2 and UKMarc standards, and this is already proving of mutual benefit to members, enabling them to make use of each other's records the more easily in their own retroconversion and current cataloguing programmes. There are already over one million records in the database, and this may almost have doubled by the end of the year. At this stage the database is still very much under development as a librarian's tool and not yet ready for wider availability nor in a form suitable for reader access, but its potential for the coordination of university research library resources in the UK can already be surmised.

The CURL initiative would have been almost impossible without the existence of the Joint Academic Network (JANET), and so would the Scottish Academic Libraries Bibliographic Information Network (SALBIN) initiative to which Edinburgh is equally committed. The Working Group on Cooperation, which meets under the auspices of the National Library of Scotland, aims in its SALBIN project to create an easy mechanism whereby a reader can search a range of library catalogues via JANET, beginning with those in his immediate locality. With welcome support first from the British Library and now from the UGC, Edinburgh University Library is overseeing the development of the software which is intended to be micro-based for use by readers themselves. The SALBIN software takes each library's catalogue as it finds it, and leads the remote reader through it, with all its idiosyncracies. It presents the reader with easy menu-driven access to his choice of catalogue. In some ways the SALBIN project and the CURL project are complementary; SALBIN makes few demands on participating libraries, requires no commitment to particular standards; it is primarily a reader's tool.

A research library cannot always wait for emerging standards. Readers are importunate and information must be provided speedily. The confusion of standards for CD-ROM publications is viewed by the Computing Service with suspicion, but the Library is as unable to resist such publications as it is to resist volumes which do not conform to the octavo norm. CD-ROM systems are in use on several sites not only for bibliographical reference but for full text searching and manipulation: the IBYCUS database holding the corpus of ancient Greek literature was the first to be installed, in the Theology Library. But the major disadvantage of CD-ROM publications in a dispersed library is that they cannot be 'networked'; to make the data available on two sites one must buy it twice. Not until CD-ROM-based data can be accessed across a network will their potential be fully exploited.

The problem of access to proprietary data is perhaps the most intransigent of the issues facing the research library today. With the development of image transmission and optical scanning, the scope for storing and transmitting the texts of works in heavy demand for use by a number of readers at a time, or maybe in homes, offices or laboratories even when the Library is closed, opens up vistas of a new level of service which could not be realised hitherto. But the intractable issue of copyright looms large at present. One can only hope that site licences will be available in future, and that universities themselves will collaborate in the archiving of texts in electronic form and make them available over JANET, if only as a preservation measure.

Control of access is going to be crucial in the fully developed electronic campus, if confidentiality, copyright and the integrity of data are to be preserved. This will be a university problem, to be solved by faculties and academic services together. However good the automatic controls, human intervention will be needed to monitor and review.

The implications of the electronic campus for human resources are already emerging. Enhanced facilities bring increased demand, and savings in transaction costs are counterbalanced by the increase in transactions. The management of an integrated database for a large university library is far more demanding than the creation of separate local catalogues to local standards. At Edinburgh it has been necessary to create two new staff divisions – Automated Systems and Database Control – against a background of severe pressure on staff resources, over 30% of academic-related posts having been lost since the decade began – and any hope that they would be needed for the duration of the systems implementation and the retroconversion programme alone has long since been banished.

The resource implications for the recurrent cost of library operations are also huge. An increasing proportion of the non-staff budget must be spent on systems maintenance. All too often this must be at the expense of books and journals for which, as publication increases, demand continues to rise. At Edinburgh maintenance of computer systems and network costs now account for about 10% of total non-staff recurrent costs. This is cause for some concern, and the Library must seek every possible economy.

But with fuller use of the collections, every pound spent on them gives better value for money. If research libraries are able to maintain their principle of free mutual access not only to catalogues collaboratively created but also to collections collaboratively developed and preserved, the researcher will gain immeasurably, not only from his own university's investment in an electronic campus, but from the new network environment in which the research library can best fulfil its role as a national resource.

103

Case Study: Leicester Polytechnic

Mel Collier, *Leicester Polytechnic*

Introduction

As early as 1979 proposals were made at Leicester Polytechnic to move away from the conventional computer centre towards a distributed computing system via a campus network. This proposal anticipated the vast changes which would take place in the 1980s in computer power and cost and can be seen now as a bold and imaginative step given that many computer centre managers were defensive and dismissive of such ideas. Today Leicester Polytechnic is operating a distributed computing strategy and has perhaps travelled further down the road of distributed computing than any other higher education institution in the UK. This paper outlines the background to the strategy, describes present systems in place and discusses plans and issues for the future.

Background to the strategy

Leicester is a large polytechnic with nearly a third of its students in mainstream IT disciplines. IT permeates most courses. The Polytechnic has a city centre campus and a county campus some six miles from the city centre. The main computing facility until 1986 was a Burroughs 6800 mainframe situated in the Computer Centre. Additionally, there was a large number of micros and minis scattered around the Polytechnic which were owned by individual departments or projects and were not communal resources. The distributed computer strategy evolved over a number of years out of the tentative proposals made in 1979, resulting in a policy document in 1984. The main stimulus for the debate was the need to replace an obsolescent mainframe with facilities which would most closely serve the very diverse computing needs of the Polytechnic departments. From the outset the academic community had a strong voice in determining the policy and not just those academics who might be regarded as in mainstream IT disciplines. In this user-driven and very lively debate the following issues emerged as being essential to the strategy:

- Choice of computing equipment should be determined by user need and application.

- Centralised mainframe-type provision is inherently inflexible, expensive and inappropriate for a diverse computing environment.

- Equipment purchased with central Polytechnic funds should nevertheless be subject to Polytechnic policy.

- Departments or project staff should be free to make decisions about purchases from their own funds.

- Much student course and project work could be carried out on low-cost micros, freeing larger machines for advanced and specialist work. Well over 1000 workstations were envisaged.

- Interconnection of facilities would be required for internal information transfer and external links.

The strategy

In January 1985 it was determined that future investment would be according to the distributed computing strategy. The immediate priority was to replace the Burroughs 6800 and at the very least maintain the work carried out on that facility. The main components of the strategy are:

- A node system initially of seven academic nodes based in major buildings, plus the Library node and the Administration node. These are funded from central resources and are part of the general computing resource. Notwithstanding, equipment is chosen according to local need and ranges from laboratories of IBM PC clones to advanced facilities.

- Departmental facilities purchased from departmental or external funds, ranging from micros dedicated to departmental staff to advanced facilities.

- Interconnection of nodes and/or departmental facilities for information transfer and access to external networks and facilities such as regional computing centres. Such interconnection should be on the basis of established need.

It will be immediately noted that there is no place in this strategy for a computer centre as a physical entity, nor did the strategy specify any network infrastructure. There were implications, therefore, for the management and staffing of a computing service which will be mentioned below. The implication for networking was that no substantial enhancement of existing infrastructure would take place until the nodes were reasonably well established and decisions would be made in the light of perceived needs at that time. The strategy was to be implemented incrementally (perhaps the main virtue of the distributed approach) and we are now in the fourth year of the policy.

Summary of established node facilities

1.	Bosworth House Node Management, Economics and Accounting	3 micro laboratories
2.	Clephan Node Architecture, Land and Building Studies	6 Apollo DN3000 1 micro laboratory
3.	Elfed Thomas Node Law, Fine Art	1 micro laboratory
4.	Fletcher Node Art and Design	Spaceward Graphics System 1 micro laboratory Industrial Design CAD facility
5.	Hawthorn Node Science and Technology Departments*	1 micro laboratory 2 Prime minis (CAD) 15 Apollo DN3000
6.	James Went Node Maths, Computing, Stats*	16 Apollo DN3000 1 micro laboratory
7.	Library Node	DG MV 4000 Database machine and library system 1 micro laboratory
8.	Scraptoft Campus Node Humanities, Social Science, Education, Life Sciences, Speech Pathology, Performing Arts	1 micro laboratory
9.	Administration Node	Pyramid work centre

* These departments also have substantial departmental facilities.

Existing campus network infrastructure

The heart of the Polytechnic campus-wide computer network is a closed loop of cable connecting parts of the Went, Clephan and Hawthorn buildings. Other parts of these buildings, and other buildings, are connected to this loop or ring by other cables (or lines). Links to other local area networks in the Polytechnic and to external networks make up the rest of the campus network. The network also provides access to certain services outside the Polytechnic, for example the academic network JANET. Through JANET, authorised researchers can communicate with computers at other polytechnics and universities. The current state of the Polytechnic network is shown in Figure 1. To use the network you must have access to either (a) a terminal (or a microcomputer with software to enable it to act as a terminal) which is connected directly to the network, or (b) a terminal (or micro) connected to one of these computers attached to the network which allow terminal users to communicate with the network, e.g. the Primes in Mechanical and Production Engineering.

Although originally based on a Cambridge ring, the network now consists of a number of Packet Assembler Disassemblers (PADs) and X.25 switches. Typically a terminal or computer is connected by a synchronous line to a PAD, which is in turn connected by a synchronous, packet-based X.25 link to an X.25 switch. This switch routes messages out to other switches, and hence onto other PADS, terminals and computers. One of the switches carries the JANET link, giving access to other institutions.

Computers and services available on the network

OPAC   The On-line Public Access Catalogue on the Kimberlin Library's Data General minicomputer. Availability of all books can be checked without visiting the library. Documentation available from the Library. No usercode or password is required.

CAD/CAM   Two Prime minicomputers in the School of Mechanical and Production Engineering used for Computer-Aided Design/ Computer-Aided Manufacture.

DGEN   A Data General MV4000 in the School of Electronic and Electrical Engineering, running the DG/UX operating system, a version of UNIX.

Figure 1   Leicester Polytechnic Campus Network

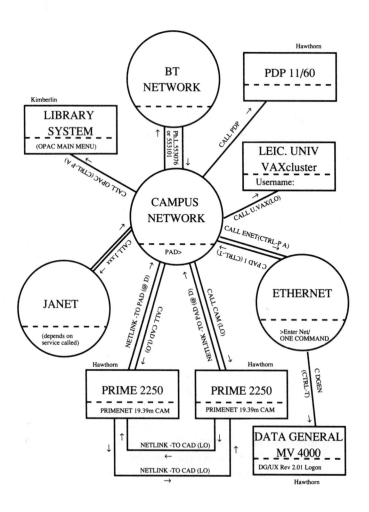

PDP   A PDP 11/60 minicomputer used for research in the School of Electronic and Electrical Engineering.

Current issues

Priority in the strategy was given to replacing and upgrading the academic (primarily teaching) computing resource after the demise of the Burroughs. That phase has now been substantially completed (except of course that demands for computing resources are never satisfied) and attention is turning to the networking infrastructure. This focuses on three main issues:

- Replacement of the private branch telephone exchange.

- Provision of a secure network for a management information system.

- Upgrade or replacement of existing infrastructure for general academic and information transfer purposes.

It is tempting to contemplate a solution for all these problems by installation of a totally integrated high speed, high capacity, multi-media network, the ideal wired-up campus concept. In reality there is considerable doubt amongst the user community that such an ambitious enterprise would be a cost-effective and reliable solution within a reasonable time span. The costs could well be prohibitive unless substantial external sponsorship were obtained and there are many technical uncertainties. It is likely that a new voice PBX will be sought which will provide maximum flexibility of interface with data systems and that sensitive systems will be restricted to a secure independent network. For general academic and information transfer applications it is widely recognised that integrated services provision for electronic mail, document delivery, information retrieval (both from the library's systems and from external networks), and transfer of information within the Polytechnic is extremely important. In a situation where computing resources are still in heavy demand, the scope for resource sharing between nodes is limited, albeit desirable in principle. Campus networking is therefore likely to concentrate on information services provision and this aim is very much assisted by a close working relationship between the library and computing services.

Information services

Leicester Polytechnic Library has carried out considerable development in the field of information services networking. LAN developments include the attachment of the online catalogue to the campus network and research into a LAN-based decision support system funded by the British Library Research and Development Department [1]. It was one of the first academic libraries to make its catalogue available by public dial-up access and via JANET. At national level it runs COPOST, the electronic mail system for libraries and the information industry, and manages LA-Net, the Library Association's electronic mail service. With this background the library service is keen to develop an integrated systems approach to information services and information transfer within the Polytechnic and has been identified as a major agent in the institution's continuing network development. Plans and proposals include the following:

- Electronic mail facilities throughout the Polytechnic.

- Distributed online searching.

- Extension of catalogue access throughout the Polytechnic.

- Document request and delivery (electronic and hard copy) to offices.

- Networked management information from the library for academic budget holders.

- Diary service.

- Text transfer and support for Polytechnic publishing.

Organisational aspects

As all polytechnics, Leicester is preparing for incorporation in April 1989. In Leicester's case the major organisational change is a rationalisation of the management structure to cope with the new responsibilities and challenges. The Polytechnic will change from a six faculty/twenty-five school structure to one with ten academic cost centres each with about three departments. Considerable management and financial responsibility will be delegated. Support services are also under review and it is likely that academic support services such as

110

libraries, computing services and educational technology will come under a single cost centre. Administrative and infrastructure support such as telephones, printing and other central services may also be grouped together. As far as academic support services are concerned it is generally agreed that technology and educational development is forcing convergence and that recognition of this in the structure is to be welcomed despite the fact that there will be short-term problems to be solved.

Conclusion

The adoption of a distributed computing strategy with its origins in the late 1970s was a bold and far-sighted step. Its implementation was driven by two predominant requirements: the need to satisfy user demand and the need to replace an obsolete facility in the most economic way. Attention is now focusing on the communications aspects of the policy with information services as the major factor in interconnection. Organisational changes are under consideration to respond to the twin imperatives of incorporation and convergence.

References

[1] Adams, R. J. & M. Collier. Local area network developments at Leicester Polytechnic Library. *Program,* 21(3), 1987, 275-82.

Where views are expressed in this paper they belong to the author, not necessarily to Leicester Polytechnic.

JANET and Academic Resource Sharing [summary of verbal presentation]

Professor Mike Wells, *University of Leeds*

Let me start my paper with a few vital statistics about JANET. There are eight switching nodes, about 125 sites, 700 systems, 20 000 terminals, and some 40 000 users sending about 1000 megabytes in messages each day. A key point about JANET is that there are no usage charges. The major expense of the network is contained in standing charges borne by the Computer Board. The philosophy is to encourage use and to ensure that as an expensive, installed service it does not stand idle because of prohibitive user charges, which would also be expensive to collect. We could treble the costs of JANET without putting usage up at all.

I want to tell you a fable for our times. Up until the mid-sixties computing meant 'doing arithmetic'. It was believed that large computers did arithmetic more cheaply and so a few big, shared computers were installed, with disks to keep them busy. But what did users do? They used the systems to store their data and then wrote editors to maintain them. They did not actually do any arithmetic except to the extent that they used the processing systems to help them maintain large volumes of data. Moving on to the mid-seventies, computing had come to mean 'doing arithmetic on data held on discs on the system'. Large computers with large discs still did this cheaply and so networks were installed to allow users access to these systems. However, although every big computer was linked into a network there was no standardisation. The plethora of non-standard networks was probably a major cause of frustration as hopes of access were raised that could not be satisfied. And what did users do? They used the systems to construct mail systems for inter-person communication! One has to conclude the obvious, namely that the imagination and skill of a group of computer users far exceeds the corporate imagination of a group of computer service suppliers. Putting in a system with a view to telling people what use to make of it is generally counter-productive, because they will all 'do their own thing', which is usually something well beyond ones wildest speculation!

There is a moral to be drawn from this fable. People only turn into users if you offer them what they want. If you do not offer what they want they will do one of three things: find someone who will; buy their own facility and work in splendid isolation; or install their own system over yours. This last action is probably more common than we know as it is virtually undetectable.

One therefore needs to ask the question, what do academics want when they share resources? Certainly the main reason is seldom cost saving! They may share if it gives them access to otherwise inaccessible resources. But what academics really relish is better contact with other academics, and the thing that really encourages sharing is when by so doing, they gain access to like-minded people working in the same broad field. In this way they can actively share results of work in a timely fashion.

In conclusion, what do we need to provide? Saving costs does not generate much interest. Access to better facilities generates a lot of interest. Better access to existing facilities generates interest and it is cheap. JANET is a fine example of this. It costs some £2 million per annum, very little in the context of a Computer Board annual budget of some £40 million, and a total universities computing budget each year of some £1500 million. The cost of JANET as a mechanism for providing better access is a very small percentage of the total. Access to effective inter-person communications is always welcome.

The Future of the Intellectual Infrastructure of the UK [summary of address to the conference]

Professor Tom Stonier, *University of Bradford*

The most important input into modern productive systems is no longer land, labour, or capital. It is know-how. This explains why the 'knowledge industry' has been the most rapidly growing sector of the economy during this century. The knowledge industry has many components. A key component is its intellectual infrastructure which includes a society's collective brain and nervous system. Among the former are included libraries, museums, archives, etc. responsible for the storage of information – i.e. a collective memory. Among the latter are included postal systems, telegraph, telephone and other forms of communication. In addition, the learning and thinking function of society's collective brain includes the education system, the mass media, and scientific research establishments.

This entire intellectual infrastructure is being dramatically upgraded as a result of the introduction of information technology. There has never been anything on this scale in previous history – both in terms of its pace, and in terms of its impact on society.

A historical parallel occurred about half a millenium ago when the printing press become established in Europe. It has long been a puzzle why, given the superiority of Chinese technology up through the middle ages, Europe began to pull ahead significantly in the late 16th and early 17th century. There are a number of contributing factors such as the rise of competing nation states and the concomitant warfare, differences in political systems, differences in religious outlook – all of these (and others) may have played a part. But none of these really can account for the European ascendancy. The development of a trans-European intellectual infrastructure can.

There were two major components to the development of this trans-European infrastructure. The first was mercantilism. Mercantilism laid the foundation for, and in turn was further reinforced by, the creation of a sophisticated transportation and communications network. Such a system also existed in China. However, European merchants, unlike their Chinese counterparts, became powerful and achieved high status. As such, merchants in Europe became major agents in technology transfer.

The second, and more important, reason was the introduction of the printing press into Europe in the 15th century. In fact, the printing press had existed in the Far East for several centuries before that. However, its usefulness was almost wholly negated by the complexity of an idiographic language – a language which could be read by only a very small number of mandarins and scholars. Still today, it takes many years of study to learn to read Chinese. In contrast, a truly phonetic language, Latin, served by an alphabet of only 26 characters could be learned in a matter of months, if not weeks. Most of the clergy and aristocracy at the time could read Latin script.

Gutenberg's press appeared in the 1440s. Within 30 years there were 236 printing presses in Italy (Venice became a major printing centre), 78 in Germany, and 68 elsewhere. By 1500 the number of printing presses in Europe had more than doubled again. During the 16th century publishing became distinct from printing. Antwerp became a centre of book publishing. Much of the early publishing related to either government edicts and affairs of state, or to religious tracts. However by the 17th century, scholarly and scientific tracts became common – the trans-European nervous system had developed a valuable adjunct to its intellectual infrastructure. Without the printing press it is unlikely that institutions like the Royal Society would ever have become effective.

The impact of computers and related information/communications technology is parallel to that of the printing press – but much more profound. Unlike computers, the printing press never got into the home – or anywhere else beyond the print shop. In contrast, the computer is invading every facet of industrial, business and personal life. Nowhere is its impact likely to be more profound that in the education system itself.

The lecture will address itself to the role of computers in education in general, then describe the current efforts to computerise totally Bradford University – and in due course, the entire British higher education system. Any institution of higher education which does not train its students to become fully conversant with computers (that does not mean programming them) is not doing its job!

Finally, the most valuable asset a country – or a company has – is its human capital – the skill and education of its people. IT is a technology which allows people to extend their brain power. It is this combination – educated people coupled to a full range of IT systems – which will provide the intellectual infrastructure necessary, both for solving the problems of the next few decades, and for grasping the enormous opportunities ahead. The address will be based largely on three previous publications by the author [1].

References

[1] Stonier T. *The Wealth of Information: A Profile of Post-Industrial Economy*. London: Methuen/Thames, 1983.

Stonier T. & C. Conlin. *The Three Cs: Children, Computers and Communication*. Chichester: John Wiley & Sons, 1985.

Stonier T. Intelligence networks, overview, purpose and policies in the context of global social change. *Aslib Proceedings,* 38(9), September 1986, 269-74.

Summary of Syndicate Discussions

Teaching issues

The group focused attention on learning as well as teaching, and strongly supported the view that scholarly activities should inform and drive the strategy for, and design of, the electronic campus, rather than technology itself. There was a recognition that electronic tools should be exploited to make teaching and student learning more effective. However, care needs to be taken not to exaggerate their contribution, which can be seen as threatening to staff, who may then retreat, demoralised, to their blackboards. It is also politically naive to make exaggerated claims, for expensive and unfulfilled promises are stored and used in evidence against the funding claims and needs of higher education.

Consideration was given to the benefits that the electronic campus could bring to teaching and learning. By giving students freedom to choose when, where and how quickly to learn, through the provision of alternative means of acquiring basic skills and methodologies, the electronic campus allows more time and space for confronting 'debatable propositions' and encourages students to develop informatic skills, of how to learn and discover. By rehabilitating teaching and learning as an acceptable subject for inquiry, electronic tools have engendered an important and significant shift in attitudes and culture which may prove more fundamental to the improvement of educational experience than the more visible benefits of the electronic campus.

Academic staff have a crucial role to play in this process, and even the most reluctant of colleagues need to be encouraged to share in this electronic revolution and its benefits. People need to be persuaded that there is something in it for them – more job satisfaction, greater reward, or greater recognition. This requires an institutional strategy which gives support at the highest level for attention to be given to computers in teaching and learning, and also encourages 'bottom up' development and use of appropriately challenging software and systems in all subject areas.

Substantial investment is required for the electronic campus to become a reality, and networking is central to its effectiveness. Evaluation of costs and benefits should carefully identify both tangible and less obvious, but no less real, contributions to better teaching and learning.

Research issues

Research activity places a high premium on connectivity, particularly between campuses, nationally and internationally. Interdisciplinary research, maintaining relationships with subject peer groups, and the setting up of Interdisciplinary Research Centres, all suggest the need for increased electronic communication to handle complex information processes.

New research activities and scholarship are facilitated by IT , as well as increased productivity in output, both in terms of the potential to shorten publication timescales and in the avoidance of duplicating research already done, through greater access to, and awareness of, the literature. However, control of the seemingly relentless flow of information thus generated is a key problem, and mechanisms are needed for sifting information and pre-selection through intermediaries.

The problem is further increased through low threshold cost desk-top publishing systems and access from the academic's desk to informal, electronic, research information, which may never come into the formal publishing chain. Where, indeed, does publication begin in an electronic discussion cycle using electronic mail and bulletin board interaction? This informal contact has revolutionised the communication of research findings between peer groups and the creation of documents, which may now go through many draft and comment stages. Print declares its authorship in a way that electronic, informal communication does not; integrity of referencing and citation, and intellectual property rights, are unsolved problems.

IT is becoming all-pervasive, used in all disciplines, bringing rising costs associated with hardware and software requirements in the arts and social sciences, which have traditionally not been funded for high levels of equipment purchase. It remains to be seen whether scholars can increase their rate of absorption of the increasing body of literature, both in printed and electronic form.

Strategic issues

As background to developing a strategic approach to the electronic campus it is important to recognise that many of the barriers to development are attitudinal in nature. Some senior staff may see a threat to their power or status; administrators may be concerned about the security of their data once connected to a network which students use; others will be suspicious of ideas and systems brought in from elsewhere. To overcome resistance there needs to be widespread involvement in strategic planning for electronic developments.

Often the expectations of students for IT-based services exceed those of academics, particularly more senior staff. Both staff and students need to become productive users of the technology, and more significantly, acquire the skills to learn, find and interpret information in their discipline, using IT. Paradoxically, in times of decreasing resources for higher education, the widespread use of IT, coupled with increased support from learning resource centres in support of new teaching and learning approaches, is seen as the most likely way for institutions to flourish and improve the quality of the student educational experience.

For the electronic campus to become a widespread reality on a national level, the climate of opinion needs to be changed. A national public relations campaign is seen as appropriate, to create support for the view that to invest in IT across higher education, and to create electronic campuses, would be beneficial to the economy as a whole. There would be a very large number of intelligent users wanting access to a whole range of remote information sources, frequently supplied by the private sector. The existing network infrastructure would soon need to be extended, ideally with the provision of a very high bandwidth national network, based on fibre optic technology.

At the local level supporters of the electronic campus must know and articulate the reasons for their strategic choice, and its educational objectives. The related budgeting process should take into account changes in staffing requirements, and training, as well as ongoing costs. Recognition needs to be given to staff who involve themselves in the project, particularly to seek improvements in the teaching and learning process. Both 'top-down' and 'bottom-up' strategic approaches could be successful. Software tools and workstations need to be placed where immediate use will be made of them. An evaluation service for educational software and other tools is needed, preferably operating on a national basis. The central backbone network investment, linking buildings and central services, such as the library and the computing service, should be centrally coordinated.

Economic issues

The group addressed the question of sources of funding for the wired-up campus. There would be potential for some external funding from bodies such as the Computer Board and the Universities and Polytechnic and Colleges Funding Councils. Possible private sector sources could be tapped, but institutions needed to be wary of being tied to a single supplier and standard. However, almost certainly, these sources of funds would not be sufficient to create the full electronic campus. Additionally, there would be a need to divert existing financial resources to create the investment. This poses very real problems in a context of diminishing overall financial resources and is likely to involve painful choices, for example, if resources are to be diverted from staff to IT . Care needs to be taken to keep the institutional profile balanced.

Support was given to the policy of students buying their own microcomputers or workstations to use throughout their course, spreading the cost over several years. However, this still leaves the major onus on the institution to provide the network, data and information resource infrastructure within which the student can work electronically.

The economic justification of the electronic campus was accepted to be a difficult and intractable issue. Many of the actual benefits cannot be predicted in advance or given an absolute value. It is, however, possible to point to specific savings from present use of IT, notably in the library. Additionally, there are examples of technology increasing productivity, improving the quality of existing activities, and more importantly, opening up opportunities of doing entirely new things. It was generally agreed that there is rarely a purely economic argument for the electronic campus, but that a mix of cost and benefit justification can be made.

Organisational issues

The group focused on how an organisation can make progress on an effective IT strategy and how it might react, in structural and organisational terms, to the advance of IT . Some higher education institutions have decided to pursue a particular IT strategy and commit resources to it; others have moved forward in a more uncoordinated way. Whatever the case, there is still likely to be considerable investment in, and use of, IT.

The group fell easily into the position of preferring a clearly adopted strategy, although there is as yet little evidence to prove that institutions which have adopted clear over-arching strategies for IT have secured significant advantages over those that have not. If there is to be an IT strategy it should follow closely behind the institutional mission and academic strategy, neither of which are yet commonly articulated in the UK.

Organisational structure follows from strategic planning, and different modes are appropriate to different stages. In devising a strategy individuals are important, for their ideas and their contribution to forward thinking. In implementing the strategy a team approach, drawn from existing structures, is often suitable. To manage the system may require a change in structure. Whose role is it, for example, to make available microcomputer software for use anywhere by students? Who should be responsible in an electronic environment for all the internal information we need for our daily administrative and committee work?

Both the library and the computing centre have roles to play and vital expertise, but there needs to be some re-thinking of their relationship, and the relationship between users and central service providers. The group felt some resistance to simple mergers of academic support services. They recognised the requirement for distinctive expertise and thought that people work best in situations where they have a clear focus and professional identity. However, the need for closer relationships between such groups, and a closer identity with the academic strategy was regarded as important.

Summary of Discussion

Each session included some time for questions and comment, and the conference concluded with a plenary discussion session. The following key points were made:

- There is insufficient knowledge of how IT can be used effectively in the teaching and learning process. It is important not to lose sight of the goals of higher education and the continuing debate on how to stimulate creativity and inter-activity, and to focus on the enhancement of individual student learning and problem-solving.

- Technology is eroding the hierarchical relationship between scholars and students. Student-centred learning using IT and interactive educational software will develop students as experts, either individually or through collaborative efforts, and scholars will need to be students much of the time, to keep up with new developments and opportunities. Different kinds of interactions between the teacher and the taught will develop, because students will be able to undertake or simulate more activities using the computer, and will be able to discuss their findings from a position of more advanced understanding of concepts.

- Librarians have yet to come to terms with multimedia, and their implications for the learning experience. There are as yet very few multimedia databases, they frequently imply interdisciplinarity and multi-directional approaches, both difficult concepts for libraries. Yet they open up the most exciting educational opportunities for students. A synoptic rather than a compartmentalised view of knowledge is made possible through IT, allowing the student to synthesise knowledge and to develop individual learning paths.

- It is often difficult to persuade academics to commit time outside their specific area of research interest, to involve themselves in the wider issues that will shape the future. A good approach is to start with an identification of their information needs and to build up a genuine strategic planning activity from a large number of individual cases, to provide generalisable results.

- The CTI has achieved greatest success in projects where control of, and access to, resources has been in the hands of academic departments, with computing experts playing an entirely secondary role. The landmark projects have been created by faculty members leading teams and creating material to teach their students. This does not necessarily imply an anarchic approach, provided that an appropriate intellectual and administrative infrastructure brings together people with similar objectives, to make it possible for them to share expertise and effort in the development of educational software.

- The importance and the difficulties of cost justification of campus networking and continual investment and re-investment in IT was a recurrent theme of the conference. Concern was expressed that arguments should focus on indicators of output rather more than has generally been the case so far. It is important to establish objectives and achievements in terms of enhancement of the quality of learning, and the student product resulting from experience of the wired-up campus.

- There are a number of specific examples of increases in productivity of institutions, relating to the introduction of automation. In libraries transaction costs have in many cases gone down substantially. Livenet, the London University video network, is justifying its running costs by saving travel time of students and staff. At the University of Ulster the network and its services are cost justified through savings in travel costs, telephone charges, and improved access to management and administrative information. Often a network can be justified for one particular function, and as a by-product it will open up a range of other opportunities and facilities, which can be added at a marginal cost. Sensitively handled internal and external public relations activities are an essential part of making the case for investment.

- The systematic measurement of the value gained from IT innovation is difficult, particularly as it should involve pre- and post-innovation study. It is also likely that the environment will be changing at the same time as network implementation, for example, the institution may well experience a reduction in resources. In addition we keep on discovering that there are always unanticipated consequences of the introduction of IT, again lessening the value of comparative study. There is an increasing number of lessons becoming available from the USA on the impact and value of the electronic campus, although many are not in published form.

- Budgeting for IT should be an essential part of university and polytechnic strategic planning. It is necessary to allow not only for capital costs, but also for maintenance and for an increasingly short investment cycle. It is difficult to come to terms with such an item which is growing to be a very substantial fraction of any university budget, at the same time as overall cuts in resources are being made. It requires very careful thinking about the opportunity costs of developing IT as a central part of any university strategy. Difficult choices will have to be made, balancing IT against other demands, for example, for staff and buildings.

- There is a relationship between local planning for IT and strategies at a national level. Libraries, for example, in the UK, who choose an IT-oriented, information-focused strategy, are dependent on the British Library for access to their extensive holdings of serials.

- The development and control of information resources is becoming a key policy issue on campus. It is important not to confuse distributed computing power with distributed management power. They do not necessarily go together. The closer working of computing and library staff requires clear personnel policies, and considerable staff development effort. The cultures and expectations of each group are somewhat different and their job satisfaction tends to come in different ways.

- The first age of IT has maintained libraries as self-standing entities. This era will not be repeated, and libraries are now in a much more complex relationship with other IT and service suppliers on the campus. To avoid becoming cut off from mainstream activities it is important for the library and the librarian to become centrally involved in networking strategy.

- Strongly differing views were expressed on the future use of video on campus. Some saw it having a positive place for lecture review, time-shifting of lectures for part-time students, extension of education via distance learning, through satellite and cable transmission, and so on. The market for distance learning is likely to increase substantially, to update professional and other skills into the 1990s.

- The complementary nature of CD-ROM technology and the use of online databases was discussed in detail. It was felt that publishers were still looking for the best application of CD-ROMs and were in the early stages of developing their strategies for electronic publishing, particularly beyond purely bibliographic products. The problems of cost control, especially when searching results in requests for hard copy or electronic document supply, were raised.

- Cooperation is needed between publishers and academics on the question of adding value to electronic products, rather than merely replicating the deficiencies of stiffly printed and formatted documents on disk. This requires the more general use of standard mark-up codes and the engineering of a more flexible concept of text publishing, including facilities for users to interact with the data in unpredictable ways. As long as IT is used simply to repeat what is already on printed paper it has little future. The video-disk seems to be finding a renaissance in its use for training applications.

- An important issue is that of the place of locally accessed data on the campus. This may be through a variety of routes – CD-ROM, site licences for software and systems, centrally held files – all have a place and need to be integrated to provide the most appropriate services to users.

Sir Peter Swinnerton-Dyer concluded the conference by emphasising the importance of clarity about the concept of the electronic campus and of promoting developments in the best light. He anticipated that the network highways will be used in ways that will surprise us all. He encouraged librarians to become more integrally involved in the IT strategy of their institutions and for short-term developments to be set in the context of long-term visions and objectives.

Select Bibliography

Compiled by Margaret Mann

Adams, R. J. The network – so near yet so far away. *Netlink,* 4(1), January 1988, 7-11.

> An account of developments at Leicester Polytechnic.

Adams, R. J. & M. Collier. Local area network developments at Leicester Polytechnic Library. *Program,* 21(3), 1987, 275-82.

Advisory Board for the Research Councils, Computer Board for Universities and Research Councils and University Grants Committee. *Future facilities for advanced research computing: report of a joint working party.* Science and Engineering Research Council, 1985.

> The terms of reference of the working party were 'to consider and report on the likely needs for advanced research computing and on the various options open ... for acquiring, operating and providing access to the necessary services.' Recommendations include a national strategy.

Alty, J. Computers for every student in Strathclyde University plan. *Strathclyde University News Release,* 14 January 1985, 4.

Atack, C. Driving IT home. *Educational Computing,* 9(2), March 1988, 36-7.

> A description of Project Granta at Cambridge University, aimed at providing a network of computers throughout the university.

Bell, S. *Electronic information systems analysis: present and future information systems use by academics involved in development studies.* University of East Anglia, School of Development Studies, 1985.

Brady, P. R. & R. Startup. Expanding student access to computer facilities – the way forward? *University Computing,* 10(2), June 1988, 86-91.

> An experiment at University College Swansea to provide computing facilities in student residences.

Brindley, L. J. *Libraries and the wired-up campus: the future role of the library in academic information handling.* British Library, 1987. (British Library Research and Development Report 5953)

Report of a study visit to eight campuses in the US.

Brindley, L. J. Planning for library and information services over a campus-wide network. *Netlink,* 3(3), May 1987, 4-10.

Plans at Aston University.

Brindley, L. J. The wired-up campus and the future of the information service. *Library Association Information Technology Group Newsletter,* 15, January 1988.

Building. Widest CAD network for university. *Building,* 22 February 1985, 62.

News item about Bradford University's large order of a network for four engineering departments.

Buxton, A. JANET and the librarian. *Electronic Library,* 6(4), August 1988, 250-63.

Describes the facilities available.

Broadway, A. P. *Campus computing strategies for the 1990s.* M.Sc. thesis, Loughborough University, 1988.

Discusses the impact of computers on the curriculum, strategies for introducing computers in higher education, and possible future developments.

Cimbala, D. J. The scholarly information center: an organizational model. *College and Research Libraries,* 48(5), September 1987, 383-98.

Discusses the combination of university libraries and computer centres.

Collier, M. & D. Piper. Multi-site library networking: experience of the Polytechnic of Central London. *Program,* 18(2), April 1984, 147-56.

Computer Board for Universities and Research Councils. *Report of a working party on computer facilities for teaching in universities.* 1983.

Gardner, N. Integrating computers into the university curriculum. *Computers and Education,* 12, 1988, 23-7.

Gardner, N. No more than a tool. *The Times Higher Education Supplement,* 815, 17 June 1988, vi.

Greenwood, D. (ed.) *Scholarly communication in the electronic age.* British Library, 1986. (British Library Research and Development Report 5885)

Report of a seminar.

Hartley, D. F. The university computing service in the late 1980s. *University Computing,* 8(1), 1986, 20-5.

Examines the future of the service as networking increases.

Heeks, R. *Computerisation in academic departments: a survey of current practice.* Taylor Graham, 1987.

Holligan, P. J. *Access to academic networks.* Taylor Graham, 1986.

Holligan, P. J. Access to UK academic networks. *Information Processing and Management,* 22(4), 1986, 353-6.

A brief account of the research reported in the previous item.

Katzen, M. The impact of computers. In M. Katzen. & S. M. Howley. *Recent initiatives in communication in the humanities.* British Library, 1984, 31-3. (Library and Information Research Report 11)

Describes some developments in campus networks in the US.

Katzen, M. *Technology and communication in the humanities: training and services in universities and polytechnics in the UK.* British Library, 1985. (Library and Information Research Report 32.)

Includes the availability and use of computers in the humanities.

Kiesler, S. B. & L. S. Sproull (eds). *Computing and change on campus.* Cambridge University Press, 1987.

Lewis, M. G. Searching, storing, managing and communicating: going online via JANET using the campus VAX computer. In *Proceedings of the 11th International Online Information Meeting, London,* 8-10 December 1987, 467-75.

Experiences at Sussex University.

Manson, P. Towards the implementation of an integrated library system: the introduction of LIBERTAS at the Polytechnic of Central London. *Vine,* 65, December 1986, 3-13.

Martyn, J. *Literature searching habits and attitudes of research scientists.* British Library, 1986. (British Library Research Paper 14)

Includes the use of computerised services.

Miall, D. (ed.) *Evaluating the impact of information technology in the arts and humanities.* CTISS/CNAA, 1988.

Moon, B. E. *Report of the conference on information resources for the campus on the future, Wingspread, June 22-24, 1986.* British Library, 1986. (British Library Research and Development Report 5940)

Norton, H. Competing requirements. *The Times Higher Education Supplement,* 14 March 1985, 28, 30.

Problems facing university computing centres, including difficulties with networks.

Roberts, M. M. Campus networking strategies: an introduction. *EDUCOM Bulletin,* 23(1), Spring 1988, 13-19.

Santinelli, P. Quartet's key change. *The Times Higher Education Supplement,* 11 April 1986, 11.

A description of the QUARTET project, supported by the British Library Research and Development Department, with the aim of developing an integrated information and communication system.

SCONUL. Networking, consortia and distributive cataloguing. In *Issues facing academic libraries*. 1985, 45-51.

Report of a survey of SCONUL libraries.

Shackel, B. & D. J. Pullinger. *BLEND-1: background and developments*. British Library, 1984. (Library and Information Research Report 29)

The first of a series of reports on an experimental electronic communication system organised by Birmingham and Loughborough Universities.

Stonier, T. Total computerisation: not if but when. *Fleece* (Bradford University student magazine), May 1987.

Tuck, B. Computer networks on campus. *Netlink,* 1(2), January 1985, 4-7.

Networks available at University College London.

Van Houweling, D. The information network: its structure and role in higher education. *Library Hi-Tech,* 5(2), Summer 1987, 7-17.

Includes a description of a powerful network for an institution, designed to overcome the problems of decentralisation.

Weiskel, T. C. University libraries, integrated scholarly information systems (ISIS), and the changing character of academic research. *Library Hi-Tech,* 6(4), 1988, 7-27.

Appendix A   List of Speakers and Delegates

Speakers

Ms Lynne Brindley	Director, Library and Information Services, and Pro-Vice-Chancellor for Information Technology, Aston University
Mr Rowland C W Brown	President, OCLC Inc
Mr Mel Collier	Chief Librarian, Leicester Polytechnic
Mr Nigel Gardner	Director, ERSC Programme on Information and Communication Technologies University of Oxford (formerly head of the Computers in Teaching Initiative Support services (CTISS), Bath University)
Professor Robert Hayes	Dean, Graduate School of Library and Information Science, University of California
Professor Neil McLean	Acting Head of Computing and Library Services, Polytechnic of Central London
Professor Jack Meadows	Head, Department of Library and Information Studies, Loughborough University

Miss Brenda Moon	Librarian, University of Edinburgh
Mr Bernard Naylor	Librarian, University of Southampton
Mr Ivan Sidgreaves	Assistant Director, Plymouth Polytechnic
Professor Tom Stonier	Chairman, Postgraduate School of Studies in Science and Society, University of Bradford
Mr David Summers	Chairman, Butterworth (Telepublishing) Ltd
Sir Peter Swinnerton-Dyer	Chairman, University Grants Committee (Chief Executive Designate of the University Funding Council)
Professor Mike Wells	Director, Computing Service, University of Leeds (formerly Director of JANET)

Delegates

Professor Michael Anderson	Dean, University of Edinburgh, Faculty of Social Science
Miss Elizabeth Barraclough	Executive Director, Computing Laboratory, University of Newcastle-upon-Tyne
Dr A O Betts	Principal, Royal Veterinary College, London
Dr Clive Booth	Director, Oxford Polytechnic

Mr David Brown	Library Planning, Blackwell Group
Dr Michael Brown	Deputy Director, Leicester Polytechnic
Professor Gordon Bull	Dean, Faculty of Information Technology, Brighton Polytechnic
Mr R J Bull	Deputy Director, Plymouth Polytechnic
Professor Sir Frederick Crawford	Vice-Chancellor, Aston University
Ms Shirley Day	British Library, Research and Development Department
Professor Wallace Ewart	University of Ulster at Jordanstown
Dr Malcolm Frazer	Director and Chief Executive, CNAA
Professor Warren Gilchrist	Head, Applied Statistics and Operational Research, Sheffield City Polytechnic
Miss Maureen Grieves	Assistant Director, British Library, Research and Development Department
Mr Warren J Haas	President, Council on Library Resources, Washington, DC

Dr Edward J Herbert	Secretary, Computer Board for Universities, Department of Education and Science
Dr Gordon R Higginson	Vice-Chancellor, University of Southampton
Mr David House	Assistant Director, Brighton Polytechnic
Professor R J Hynds	Head, Imperial College Computer Centre
Professor Michael Kelly	Head, Department of French, University of Southampton
Dr Peter Kemp	Director, The Computing Service, University of Glasgow
Professor Frank E Knowles	Head, Modern Languages, Aston University
Mr Derek Law	Librarian, King's College, London
Mr Louis Lee	Head, Computer Centre, Kingston Polytechnic
Mr John Lindley	Director, Computer Centre, University of Durham
Professor Peter E Linington	Computing Laboratory, University of Kent at Canterbury
Mr Anthony Loveday	Secretary, Standing Conference of National and University Libraries

Mr Peter MacDonald	Department of Trade and Industry
Mr Graham Mackenzie	Librarian, University of St Andrews
Ms Karen Merry	Project Manager, British Library, Research and Development Department
Professor Roger Needham	Computer Laboratory, University of Cambridge
Mr Brian Perry	Director, British Library, Research and Development Department
Dr William Stubbs	Chief Executive Designate, Polytechnics and Colleges Funding Council
Mr Philip Walters	Senior Assistant Secretary, Thames Polytechnic
Mr Peter Williams	Deputy Director, Computing Service, University of Edinburgh

Appendix B   Conference Programme

Friday 28 October

16.30   Registration at Whately Hall Hotel
onwards

19.00   Sherry reception to meet speakers and delegates

19.30   Dinner and welcome by Mr Brian Perry, Director of the
British Library Research and Development Department

Saturday 29 October

09.00   Introduction: Sir Peter Swinnerton-Dyer, Chairman of
UGC

09.15   Chairman's comments: Mr W J Haas, President, Council
on Library Resources, Washington

    (i) Higher Education and the Influence of Information
Technology: Teaching. Mr N Gardner, Director of
ESRC's Programme on Information and
Communications Technologies

    (ii) Higher Education and the Influence of Information
Technology: Research. Professor A J Meadows,
Head of Department of Library and Information
Studies, Loughborough University of Technology

    (iii) 'Brushstrokes in flight': A Strategic Overview of
Trends in Technology in Higher Education. Mr R
C W Brown, President, Online Computer Library
Center, Ohio

    (iv) Strategic Overview of Information Resources in
Higher Education. Professor R Hayes, Dean of the
Graduate School of Library and Information
Science, University of California, Los Angeles

Discussion followed by coffee

11.00 Chairman's comments: Sir Frederick Crawford,
Vice-Chancellor, Aston University

 (i) The Changing Economics of Information: an
Industry View. Mr D Summers, Chairman,
Butterworth (Telepublishing) Ltd

 (ii) The Changing Economics of Information: a
Library/Information Service View. Professor N
McLean, Head of Computing and Library
Services, Polytechnic of Central London

 (iii) Organisational Issues. Mr I Sidgreaves, Assistant
to the Director, Plymouth Polytechnic

Discussion followed by lunch

14.00 Chairman's comments: Professor Needham, Computer
Laboratory, University of Cambridge

 (i) Case studies – reports on key issues and progress
in four environments representing different types
of higher education institution
  (a) Southampton University. Mr B Naylor
  (b) Aston University. Ms L Brindley
  (c) Edinburgh University. Miss B Moon
  (d) Leicester Polytechnic. Mr M Collier

Each speaker will examine the following topics
from the point of view of their own institution: the
position of libraries in the new environment;
institutional and library policies; strategic plans;
organisational change; and resource implications.

 (ii) JANET and academic resource sharing. Professor
M Wells, University of Leeds Computing Service

Discussion followed by tea

16.00- Syndicate discussions. Five groups will be formed to
17.30   develop and discuss the relevant points raised earlier in
        the day in the presented papers.

19.00   Dinner

20.30   The future of the intellectual infrastructure of the UK.
        Professor T. Stonier, Postgraduate School of Studies in
        Science and Society, University of Bradford

Sunday 30 October

09.30   Chairman's comments: Dr G R Higginson,
        Vice-Chancellor, University of Southampton

Reports from syndicate groups

Discussion followed by coffee

11.00   Chairman's comments: Mr Brian Perry, Director, British
        Library Research and Development Department

Plenary session: an open forum to reflect on and discuss the points and issues
raised throughout the conference

12.00   Policy issues arising. Summary of the weekend by Sir
        Peter Swinnerton-Dyer

Lunch

Disperse

Other reports

Library and Information Research (LIR) Reports may be purchased from the British Library Publications Sales Unit, Boston Spa, Wetherby, West Yorkshire LS23 7BQ, UK. Details of some other LIR Reports are given below.

LIR Report 34. Ritchie, Sheila. *Training and management development in librarianship.* 1988. pp 96. ISBN 0 7123 3049 6.

The main aim of this study was to investigate individual attitudes to career development and training, setting these in the context of training provided by libraries. Specifically, the study sought to identify any barriers to training and development and to concentrate on librarians and information workers currently belonging to the Library Association.

LIR Report 61. Best, Ron, Heyes, Susan A and Taylor, Mike. *Library provision and curriculum planning: an evaluation of the Essex Secondary Schools Education/Library Project.* 1988. pp 142. ISBN 0 7123 3127 1.

For some years the library and education services of Essex County Council have operated a grant scheme for improving library provision in the county's secondary schools. The scheme involves a rolling programme of funding on two levels. To participate in either the 'Major' or 'Minor' project, schools must demonstrate a commitment to library enhancement which is linked to curriculum development, and must establish appropriate mechanisms for achieving objectives. The report describes the findings of an independent evaluation which ran for two and a half years.

LIR Report 62. Lincoln, Paul. *The learning school.* 1987. pp 92. ISBN 0 7123 3135 2.

This report documents the efforts which William de Ferrers School has made to implement a 'whole school' approach to information skills. The school is a purpose-built comprehensive in a rapidly expanding new town, with which it shares its library. The quality of the library was the initial stimulus to the school's concern with information skills but interest subsequently broadened under the influence of external advisers. The report highlights the difficulties of reconciling a whole school approach with the demands of examination syllabuses and the drive to develop strong subject departments, at the same time showing evidence of a developing discussion, involving pupils as well as teachers, about the process of learning.

LIR Report 63. Valentine, Pearl and Nelson, Brian. *Sneaky teaching: the role of the school librarian – teachers' and school librarians' perceptions*. 1988. pp 131. ISBN 0 7123 3139 5.

The authors examine teachers' and school librarians' perceptions of the role of the school librarian, to see how much they differ and to what extent they are affected by the teaching style of the school, the appointment of qualified librarians to school libraries, the presence of new technology in the library and the administrative relationship between the school library support service and the education department. A comparative study was made in three local authority areas. Recommendations include checklists for teachers and school librarians, intended to foster closer relationships and better use of libraries, as well as a statement for local education authority and school management teams on the most effective means of staffing, equipping and administering school libraries.

LIR Report 64. Dover, Marilyn. *Public Information in Rural Areas: Technology Experiment (PIRATE)—Part I*. 1988. ISBN 0 7123 3143 3.

PIRATE has as its theme the exploration of technologies to overcome difficulties in finding community information. The technologies chosen provide a very useful means of collecting data in an orderly fashion and facilitating public access. A Torch microcomputer forms the crux of the system and has attached to it an ALS Browser, which provides touch-screen access to the databases held on the Torch. dBASE II provides the retrieval mechanism.

LIR Report 65. Williamson, Robin. *Knowledge Warehouse*. 1987. pp 65. ISBN 0 7123 3145 X.

The Knowledge Warehouse is a national archive of works deposited in electronic form. The report describes the technical, legal and commercial aspects of the Warehouse. Technical issues include discussion of the process of capturing electronic versions of works, the archive storage medium, standards issues and the creation of a detailed index to the archive. Legal issues include the establishment of an archive trust, ownership and control of archived data, copyright and conditions for deposit of works. Commercial issues include exploitation of archived data, types of product to emerge from the archive and key contractual issues.

LIR Report 66. Vickery, A, Brooks, H M, Robinson, B A and Stephens, J. Consultant: Vickery, B C. *Expert system for referral.* 1988. pp 245. ISBN 0 7123 3146 8.

This report describes a three-year project, carried out at the University of London to develop an expert system (ES) for referral. Before the project began, the then existing ES shells were investigated, but found to be lacking in sophistication for a referral tool. A prototype was built in the field of horticulture and many sources of material were entered into the system. A user-friendly interface was developed, and the system was adapted to run on Sirius and IBM-AT microcomputers. Full details of every stage of system building and evaluation are contained in the report.

LIR Report 67. Sanger, Jack (ed). *Teaching, handling information and learning.* 1989. pp 374. ISBN 0 7123 3147 6.

The project described in this report set out to investigate information handling in its broadest sense, across a wide spectrum of pupil age and curriculum subject. The methodology used was that of action research. A group of teachers from various parts of the educational system met regularly throughout the project and were encouraged to investigate classroom issues of concern to them. The project team, at the University of East Anglia, provided support in the form of observation, feedback and data collection but tried to avoid imposing any 'agenda' on the group members. The final report offers a wide variety of perspectives on attempts to develop more 'pupil-centred' approaches to learning.

LIR Report 68. Galpin, Barrie and Schilling, Mike. *Computers, topic work and young children: learning to use information in the primary classroom.* 1988. pp 150. ISBN 0 7123 3161 1.

The widespread availability of microcomputers in primary and middle schools presents an opportunity for pupils and teachers to explore ways in which the new technology can help with information processing. By encouraging the appropriate use of microcomputers the researchers were able to improve the teaching and learning of information skills in the primary sector. A lot of the topic-based or project work in primary schools brings children into close contact with the world outside their classes. Their learning about this world and their work with microcomputers were beneficially brought together using the facilities provided by the microcomputer. They were able to store, organise and analyse the information learned and collected. The work, which was based on the use of the language PROLOG, enabled the researchers to present a package to schools which children found easy to use and adaptable to their needs.

LIR Report 69. Heeks, Peggy. *School libraries on the move: managing library change in English local authorities.* 1988. pp 72. ISBN 0 7123 3166 2.

This is a review of secondary school library development in 83 English local education authorities, with case studies of nine of these. Particular attention is paid to Berkshire, where Peggy Heeks was coordinator of the Berkshire Libraries for Learning project 1985–87. The focus throughout is the local education authority's role in the management of change, and the conditions and strategies which advance educational change.